任何值得做的，就把它做好。到头来，你活了多少岁不算什么，重要的是，你是如何度过这些岁月的。

Whatever is worth doing is worth doing well、In the end, it's not the years in your life that count、It's the life in your years.

成长是不可替代的事

牛小蹊/编译

江苏人民出版社

图书在版编目（CIP）数据

成长是不可替代的事：英汉对照 / 牛小蹊编译．-- 南京：江苏人民出版社，2016.1
ISBN 978-7-214-17086-6

Ⅰ．①成… Ⅱ．①牛… Ⅲ．①英语－汉语－对照读物 Ⅳ．① H319.4

中国版本图书馆 CIP 数据核字（2015）第 311087 号

书　　名	成长是不可替代的事：英汉对照
编 译 者	牛小蹊
责任编辑	朱　超
装帧设计	浪殿设计　飞　扬
版式设计	张文艺
出版发行	凤凰出版传媒股份有限公司 江苏人民出版社
出版社地址	南京市湖南路1号A楼，邮编：210009
出版社网址	http://www.jspph.com http://jsrmcbs.tmall.com
经　　销	凤凰出版传媒股份有限公司
印　　刷	北京中印联印务有限公司
开　　本	718 毫米 ×1000 毫米 1/16
印　　张	12
字　　数	153 千字
版　　次	2016 年 5 月第 1 版　2016 年 5 月第 1 次印刷
标准书号	978-7-214-17086-6
定　　价	24.00元

Growth Can Not Be Replaced

成长是不可替代的事

成长是严肃的，有时还会很糟糕——但你依然可以乐观向上充满希望，迎着挫折一路向前。别忘了答应自己要做的事情，别忘了答应自己要去的地方，否则，生命又有什么意义呢?

True Nobility
真正的高贵

◎ Ernest Hemingway

In a calm sea every man is a pilot. But all sunshine without shade, all pleasure without pai—is not life at all. Take the lot of the happiest—it is a tangled yarn. Bereavements and blessings, one following another, make us sad and blessed by turns. Even death itself makes life more loving. Men come closest to their true selves in the sober moments of life, under the shadows of sorrow and loss. In the affairs of life or of business, it is not intellect that tells so much as character, not brains so much as heart, not genius so much as self-control, patience, and discipline, regulated by judgment. I have always believed that the man who has begun to live more seriously within begins to live more simply without. In an age of extravagance and waste, I wish I could show to the world how few the real wants of humanity are. To regret one's errors to the point of not repeating them is true repentance. There is nothing noble in being superior to some other man. The true nobility is in being superior to your previous self.

风平浪静的大海上，每个人都是领航员。但是，只有阳光而无阴影，只有欢乐而无痛苦，那就不是人生。以最幸福的人的生活为例——它是一团纠缠在一起的麻线。丧亲之痛和幸福祝愿，彼此相接，让我们一会儿伤心一会儿高兴。甚至死亡本身也会使生命更加可亲。在人生的清醒时刻，在哀痛和伤心的阴影之下，人们与真实的自我最接近。在人生或者职业的各种事务中，性格的作用比智力大得多，头脑的作用不如心情，天资不如由判断力所节制着的自制、耐心和规律。我始终相信，开始在内心生活得更严肃的人，也会在外表上开始生活得更朴素。在一个奢华浪费的年代，我希望能向世界表明，人类真正需要的东西是非常之少的。悔恨自己的错误，而且力求不再重蹈覆辙，这才是真正的悔悟。优于别人，并不高贵。真正的高贵应该是优于过去的自己。

目 录 | CONTENTS

爱恋初开的季节

梦想的袅袅回音

CONTENTS 目录

一起走过的日子

重新遇见自己

Chapter 1

爱恋初开的季节

I'm just a sunflower, waiting for my only sunshine.

我只是一朵向日葵，等待着属于我的唯一的阳光。

Dawning of Love
情窦初开

◎ Ivan Turgenev

I seized the opportunity when she looking down and fell to watching her, at first **stealthily**[①], then more and more boldly. Her face struck me as even charming as on the previous evening; everything in it was so delicate, clever, and sweet.

She was sitting with her back to a window covered with a white blind, the sunshine, streaming in through the blind, shed a soft light over her **fluffy**[②] golden curls, her innocent neck, her sloping shoulders, and tender rising bosom. I gazed at her, and how dear and near she was already to me! It seemed to me I had known her a long while and had never known anything or lived at all till I met her.

She was wearing a white dress; I would gladly, I felt, have kissed every fold of that dress. The tips of her little shoes peeped out from under her skirt.

"And here I am sitting before her," I thought, "I have made acquaintance with her. What happiness, my God!"

① stealthily ['stelθili] adv. 暗地里，偷偷摸摸地
② fluffy ['flʌfi] adj. 蓬松的，松软的

美丽语录

When the words "I love you" were said by you for the first time, my world blossoms.

第一次听到你对我说"我爱你"，我的世界一瞬间鲜花绽开。

我抓住了机会，就在她低头的时候，我看了她一眼。起初是偷偷地看，后来就越来越大胆。她的面孔是如此精致，散发着聪慧和甜美，看起来比昨晚更加迷人，深深地触动了我的心。

她背对着窗子坐在那里，窗上挂着白色的窗帘，阳光透过窗帘射进屋里。她蓬松的金色卷发、洁白无瑕的脖颈、瘦削的肩膀和微微隆起的胸脯都沐浴着柔和的阳光。我目不转睛地看着她，现在，我和她是如此亲近！我感觉自己在很久以前就认识她，并且在遇到她之前，好像什么也不知道，根本意识不到自己的存在。

她身穿一条白色连衣裙，裙子下面隐约可见她那小巧的鞋尖。我感到自己非常乐意去亲吻那条裙子的每一个褶皱。

"我就坐在她的面前，"我的脑中萦绕着这样的想法，"我与她已经相识了，上帝，我感到特别幸福！"

我几乎无法压抑内心的喜悦，差一点就从椅子上跳了起来。然而，我

I could hardly keep from jumping up from my chair in **ecstasy**[①], but I only swung my legs a little like a small child who has been given sweets.

I was happy as a fish in water, and I could have stayed in that room for ever, have never left that place.

Her eyes were slowly lifted, and once more her clear eyes shone tenderly upon me, and again she smiled.

"How you look at me!" she said shyly, holding up a finger.

I blushed. "She understands it all and see it all," flashed through my mind. "And how could she fail to understand and see it all?"

① ecstasy ['ekstəsi] n. 狂喜；出神，入迷

只是像一个得到糖果的小孩子，微微地摆动着双腿。

我觉得很快乐，就像水中游来游去的小鱼儿。我真想永远也不要离开那个地方，永远待在那个房间里。

她慢慢地抬起眼睛，清澈的目光再次温柔地落在了我身上，她再一次冲着我嫣然而笑。

她竖起一根手指，害羞地说："你为什么一直看着我？"

我的脸一下子涨红了，脑海中闪现出这样的想法："她明白了一切，也看到了一切。她怎么会不明白，怎么会看不到呢？"

Speak Out Your Love
勇敢说出你的爱

◎ Anonymous

There was once a guy who suffered from cancer, a cancer that can't be cured. He was 18 years old and he could die anytime. All his life, he was **stuck in**① his house being taken cared by his mother. He never went outside but he was sick of staying home and wanted to go out for once. So he asked his mother and she gave him permission.

He walked down his block and found a lot of stores. He passed a CD store and looked through the front door for a second as he walked. He stopped and went back to look into the store. He saw a beautiful girl about his age and he knew it was love at first sight. He opened the door and walked in, not looking at anything else but her. He walked closer and closer until he was finally at the front desk where she sat.

She looked up and asked, "Can I help you?"

She smiled and he thought it was the most beautiful smile he has ever seen before and wanted to kiss her right there.

He said, "Uh... Yeah... Umm... I would like to buy a CD."

---

① stick in 在家

美丽语录

Love is... when you've had a huge fight but then decide to put aside your egos, hold hands and say, "I Love You".

爱是……当你作了巨大的思想斗争，最终决定抛开你的自尊，攥紧手，说出"我爱你"。

从前，有一个少年患了癌症，根本无法治愈。他只有 18 岁，而且随时都可能死去。他每天都待在家里，由母亲照顾着。他从来都不出门，但他实在厌倦了，想出去走走。他问他的母亲，母亲同意了。

他走在大街上，看到了许多商店。经过一家音像店时，他透过前门盯了一会儿。然后他停下来，又折回音像店望去。他看到了一个美丽的同龄女孩，他意识到自己对她一见钟情了。他打开门，走了进去，眼里始终只有她一个人。他不由自主地走到柜台前，走到那个女孩坐着的地方。

女孩抬起头问道："你想要点什么？"

她微笑着，他觉得这是他见过的最美的笑容，此时他最想做的就是亲吻她。

他结结巴巴地说："呃……是的……嗯……我想买一张 CD。"

He picked one out and gave her money for it.

"Would you like me to **wrap**[①] it for you?" she asked, smiling her cute smile again.

He nodded and she went to the back. She came back with the wrapped CD and gave it to him. He took it and walked out of the store.

He went home and from then on, he went to that store every day and bought a CD, and she wrapped it for him. He took the CD home and put it in his closet. He was still too shy to ask her out and he really wanted to but he couldn't. His mother found out about this and told him to just ask her. So the next day, he took all his courage and went to the store as usual. He bought a CD like he did every day and once again she went to the back of the store and came back with it wrapped. He took it and when she wasn't looking, he left his phone number on the desk and ran out...

RRRRRING!

One day the phone rang, and the mother picked it up and said, "Hello?"

It was the girl! The mother started to cry and said, "You don't know? He passed away yesterday..."

The line was quiet except for the cries of the boy's mother. Later in the day, the mother went into the boy's room because she wanted to remember him. She thought she would start by looking at his clothes. So she opened the closet.

She was face to face with piles and piles and piles of unopened CDs. She was surprised to find all these CDs and she picked one up and sat down on the bed and she started to open one. Inside, there was a CD and as she took it out of the wrapper, out fell a piece of paper. The mother picked it up and started to

① ② wrap [ræp] v. 包，裹，缠绕

他随便拿了张 CD，付钱给她。

“需要我把它包起来吗？”女孩问道，再次露出那可爱的笑容。

他点了点头。她回到后面，出来的时候，手里拿着包好的 CD，递给了他。他接过 CD，走出了商店。

他回家了。从那以后，他每天都要去那家音像店买一张 CD。女孩每次都将 CD 包好交给他，他也总是把 CD 带回去放进衣橱里。这个少年很害羞，始终不敢约她出去。他真的很想，但却不能。母亲知道这件事后，就不断地鼓励他。第二天，他终于鼓起勇气，像往常一样来到音像店，买了一张 CD，她也像往常一样，到后面去替他包起来。他接过 CD，趁她不注意时将自己的电话号码放在柜台上，然后跑了出去……

叮铃铃铃！

有一天，电话铃响了，母亲接起电话：“喂？”

是那个女孩！母亲伤心地哭了，她说：“你不知道吗？他昨天死了……”

电话线那端沉默了，只能听到母亲的哭泣声。那天晚些时候，母亲来到儿子的房间，她想好好地记住儿子。她想先看看他的衣服，于是打开了衣橱。

母亲面前是一堆堆没有拆开的包好的 CD。发现这些时她大吃一惊。她坐在床边，打开了一个包装，从包装盒中拿出 CD 时，盒里掉出一张小纸条。她捡了起来，上面写道：嗨……我觉得你真的很可爱，愿意和我一起出去吗？乔斯林。

read it. It said: Hi... I think U R really cute. Do u wanna go out with me? Love, Jocelyn.

The mother was deeply moved and opened another CD...

Again there was a piece of paper. It said: Hi... I think U R really cute. Do u wanna go out with me? Love, Jocelyn.

母亲深受感动，她又打开了另一个 CD 盒……

里面又有一张小纸条，上面都写着同样的话：嗨……我觉得你真的很可爱，愿意和我一起出去吗？乔斯林。

My Very First Love
我的初恋

◎ Karina

Yes this may be surprising, I was only 13 years old that time. But, I don't know how or why it happened to me so early. I fell deeply in love with a guy, who I used to think was annoying 2 months ago.

It was 1997, in Chittagong, Bangladesh, my family and I have just moved to a new apartment in a new area. So, after few weeks have passed, I started going back to school, since it was during Ramadan we moved. Well, I made some new friends in the neighborhood. This girl who was always hanging out with, her name was Ivy.

One day when I was going to school, I **bumped into**[①] Ivy on the way out of my building, and she was standing next to this guy, he lived in the building right beside mine. He said "Hi" to me, and we just asked each other "how are you" and blah blah, then I had to leave. But I noticed that guy was looking at me. It was a different kind of look, look with love in his eyes. Few days later, I noticed whenever I go to school and come back from school, he is standing in his balcony, and smiling at me. If he is not around, and some of his friends see me,

① bumped into 无意中遇到，邂逅

美丽语录

Sometimes, tears is sign of unspoken happiness. And smile is sign of silent pain.

眼泪，有时候是一种无法言说的幸福。微笑，有时候是一种没有说出口的伤痛。

这可能会令人惊讶，因为那时我只有 13 岁。但是，我也不知道为什么那么早就降临到我身上。我深深地喜欢上了一个男孩，可在那之前两个月，我还认为他十分令人讨厌呢。

1997 年，在孟加拉国的吉大港，我和家人刚搬到一个新地方，住进新公寓。由于我们是在斋月搬的家，所以过了几个星期，我才重新回到学校上学。我在附近交了一些新朋友。有个女孩总和我一起出去玩，她叫艾维。

有一天，我正要去上学，刚出家门就碰到了艾维。她站在一个男孩旁边，男孩就住在我们隔壁那栋楼房里。他跟我打了声招呼，我们也只是问对方“你好吗”之类的话，之后我就离开了。但我注意到那个男孩在看我，而且是一种不一样的眼神，眼里充满爱意。几天后，我发现我每次上学放学的时候，他都会站在阳台上看着我，朝我微笑。如果他的朋友看到我，而他又不在旁边，他们就会对我喊他的名字。哦！对了，他叫马蒙。

they start to yell out his name. Oh yeah, by the way, his name was Mamun.

So, I was very annoyed by those things. And I even told Ivy to tell Mamun to stop these foolishness. After my exams were over, I had a break. So I used to go to the roof and read books to spend my time. Mamun used to come to their roof also and both roofs where so close to each other that you can just jump from one to another.

Once I was reading a book, and I noticed Mamun come to their roof and he looked at me, and smiled. Oh my god! I don't know what happened to me. That sweet smile just took me away. I smiled back at him, for the first time. I could never forget that moment. We used to smile at each other whenever we saw each other, but never had a chat. I was sure that he liked me a lot, because, anytime he would see me on the roof from his balcony, he came up to the roof right away. I fell in love with him very deeply. I was surprised that I did. The feelings I had was so beautiful and made me so happy.

Mamun did come to my roof one day to talk to me but I wanted him to go away. I didn't want anyone to see us talking. As you know, in Bangladesh rumors go around so fast. When we talked, I saw deep love in his eyes. I always smiled at him; I didn't talk to him much. Still, life was going on so wonderfully. Mamun never told me he loved me. I thought that was because, I was 5/6 years younger than him.

Very soon, I found out that me and my family are leaving Bangladesh and coming to Canada. I was **devastated**[①]. I cried all night but there was nothing to do. When Mamun found out, he asked me on the roof, if it was true. When I said yes, he asked how long will I be in Canada. The answer was maybe forever, we

---

① devastated ['devəsteitid] adj. 极其震惊的，身心交瘁的

因此，我也很讨厌这些事情。我甚至让艾维转告马蒙停止这些愚蠢的行为。考试结束后，我有个短暂的假期，所以经常会去屋顶看书打发时间。马蒙也经常去他们的屋顶，两个屋顶离得很近，你甚至可以从一个跳到另一个上面。

有一次，我正在看书，发现马蒙也来到他家的屋顶看着我笑。哦，天哪！真不知道我怎么了，他甜美的笑容竟然把我迷住了。我不禁也对他笑了，那是第一次对他笑，我永远不会忘记那一刻。以后我们每次看见对方的时候都相视而笑，但从来没说过话。我敢肯定他非常喜欢我，因为无论什么时候，只要他从阳台上看到我在屋顶，他就会马上跑上屋顶。我自己也很惊讶，我竟然深深地喜欢上了他。这种感觉是如此美妙，让我如此幸福。

一天，马蒙来到我家屋顶上跟我说话，但我想让他离开。我不想让任何人看见我们说话。你也知道，在孟加拉国流言蜚语传得很快。我们谈话时，我看到他眼神里流露出的深深的爱恋。我一直对着他微笑，并没有和他说太多话。生活照样如此奇妙地过着，马蒙从来没有告诉我他喜欢我。我想，可能是因为我比他小五六岁的原因吧。

很快，我发现我们家就要离开孟加拉国去加拿大了。我彻底心碎了。我哭了一整夜，可这也无济于事。马蒙知道后，在屋顶上问我这是不是真的。我说是，他问我在加拿大会待多久，我说可能是永远，我们打算在加拿大定居。他看起来很沮丧，只说了声“哦”，之后我告诉了他航班的日期。

were going to settle in Canada. He looked depressed, all he said was "Oh", then I told him our flight date.

The next month, it was Ramadan again. Mamun came to say goodbye to me on the roof, he was leaving to spend his Eid with his family. That day, I was so sad, I felt like I lost something very important in my life. We said goodbye to each other, he said he thinks I am such a sweet girl, he hopes I have a great life in Canada. Oh my god, I couldn't hold myself, I think my eyes became watery. I didn't want him to see that I was crying. I said "you too" and tried to smile and left the roof right away.

That was the last day I ever saw my first love. Now 4 years later, here I am in Canada. I have a guy in my life now, whom I am deeply love with after Mamun. I never lose him.

I am over Mamun now. Everytime I remember those days, looking at each other on the roof, talking, I feel really down. I wonder where he is now, if we will even meet again, I can never forget my first love.

下个月，又是9月斋月。马蒙来到屋顶上与我道别，他要去和他的家人过开斋节。那一天，我是那么的难过，我感到我失去了生命里十分重要的东西。我们互相道别后，他说他认为我是一个很讨人喜欢的女孩，祝愿我在加拿大生活愉快。哦，天哪！我几乎无法控制自己了，我想我的眼睛一定泪汪汪的。我不想让他看到我哭。说完“你也是”，我就试着笑起来，马上离开了屋顶。

那是我最后一次看到我的初恋。现在我已经在加拿大生活了4年多，我也有了男朋友，他是在马蒙之后我深爱的一个人。我绝不会失去他。

现在，我和马蒙的事已经过去了。每当我回忆起那些日子，我们在屋顶上互相望着彼此聊天，我还是感觉很难受。我不知道他现在在哪儿，我们是否还能再见面，但我永远不会忘记我的初恋。

Will You Go Out with Me

你愿意和我约会吗

◎ Joseph Gordon

Every day I **anxiously**① wait for you to get to class. I can't wait for us to smile at each other and say good morning. Some days, when you arrive only seconds before the lecture begins, I'm incredibly impatient. Instead of reading the Daily Cal, I anticipate your footsteps from behind and listen for your voice. Today is one of your late days. But, I don't mind, because after a month of **desperately**② desiring to ask you out, today I'm going to. Encourage me, because letting you know I like you seems as risky to me as skydiving into the sea.

My roommate and her boyfriend were friends for four months before their chemistries clicked. They went to movies and meals and often got together with mutual friends. They **alternated**③ paying the dinner check. "He was like a girl friend," my roommate once laughed-blushing. Men and women relax and get to know each other more easily through such friendships. Another friend of mine believes that casual dating is improving people's social lives. When she wants to let a guy know she is interested, she'll say, "Hey, let's go get a yogurt."

① anxiously ['æŋkʃəsli] adv. 焦急地；担忧地

② desperately ['despəritli] adv. 绝望地；不顾一切地，拼命地

③ alternate [ɔ:l'tə:nit] adj.（两个）交替轮流的；间隔的；供选择的

美丽语录

One of the best things in life is seeing a smile on a person's face and knowing that you put it there.

生活中最美好的一件事情是，因为你，某个人脸上洋溢着微笑。

每天，我都焦急地等待着你来上课，迫不及待地想和你彼此微笑、互道早安。有些日子，我变得很烦躁，只因为你在上课前几秒钟才走进教室。我表面上假装看着课程表，心里却期盼背后传来你的脚步声，期盼听到你的声音。就像前些日子一样，今天你又迟到了。但是，我并不介意，因为这一个月来我一直渴望与你约会，却没有机会。今天，我要实现这个愿望。鼓励我吧，因为让你知道我喜欢你，需要像从高空跳伞落入大海一样的勇气。

四个月前，我的室友和她的男友还是普通朋友，现在，他们已经坠入了情网。他们一起看电影、一起用餐，经常同彼此的朋友聚会。吃饭时，他们轮流买单。有一次，我的室友说："他就像一个女性朋友。"说这话时，她笑得脸都涨红了。这种友谊关系，男人和女人都会感觉很轻松，并且能够更容易地了解彼此。我的另一个朋友认为，轻松的约会改善了人们的社交生活。当一个女孩想让一个男孩知道她对他有好感时，她就会说："嗨，我们一起去吃奶酪吧。"

John whipped out his wallet on our first date before I could suggest we go Dutch. During our after-dinner stroll he told me he was interested in dating me on a steady basis. After I explained 1 was more interested in a friendship, he told me he would have understood has I paid for my dinner. "I've practically stopped treating women on dates," he said defensively. "It's safer and more comfortable when we each pay for ourselves." John has assumed that because I graciously accepted his treat, I was in love. He was mad at himself for treating me, and I regretted allowing him to.

Larry, on the other hand, blushed when I offered to pay for my meal on our first date. I unzipped my purse and flung out my wallet, and he looked at me as if I had addressed him in a foreign language. Hesitant, I asked politely, "How much do I owe you?" Larry muttered, "Uh, uh, you really don't owe me anything, but if you insist..."

Insist, I though, I only offered. To Larry, my gesture was a suggestion of rejection.

Sliding into his desk, he taps my shoulder and says, "Hi, Laura, what's up?"

"Good morning," I answer with nervous chills, "Hey, how would you like to have lunch after class on Friday?"

"You mean after the midterm?" he says encouragingly. "I'd love to go to lunch with you."

"We have a date." I smile.

与约翰第一次约会的时候，我还没来得及提议 AA 制，他就突然掏出钱包付了账。晚饭后散步时，他告诉我说，想和我建立稳定的约会关系。我向他解释道，我更想与他做普通朋友，他说，要是买单时我付了自己的那份，他就会明白我的意思。他辩解道："我现在与女人约会时，已经不会给她们买单了，各付各的会更加稳妥和舒服。"约翰认为我爱上他了，因为我欣然接受了他的请客。他因为给我买单而埋怨自己，我也很后悔接受了他的请客。

然而，与拉里的第一次约会，当我提出要自己买单时，他却涨红了脸。当我拉开手提包掏出钱夹时，他看着我的眼神，就好像我用外语跟他说了什么似的。我犹豫了一下，礼貌地问他："我应该付你多少钱？"拉里不好意思地说："嗯，嗯，其实你不用付钱给我，但是，如果你坚持……"

尽管如此，我还是把钱给了拉里。对拉里而言，这是我拒绝他的暗示。

拉里溜进了自己的座位，轻拍一下我的肩膀，说道："早，劳拉，你好吗？"

我猛地回过神来，紧张地答道："嗨，早上好，周五下课后愿意和我共进午餐吗？"

他兴奋地说："你的意思是期中考试之后吗？我很愿意。"

我微笑着说："那就说定了。"

Unbosoming Myself

爱的倾诉

◎ Bret Harte

I just got off the phone with you. I wish I could be there with you as you read this one, but that may be a long way off...

Sandi, I know that your heart belongs to me and you've got my heart.

All my life, I waited for that special someone who I could say those three words and mean them. I know I say them every day, and you probably think that I don't mean it. But trust me, I mean every word of it from the bottom of my heart.

You were the first person that I had a slow dance with. The first one I've ever felt this way about. The first I could ever tell such secrets to and never feel any **remorse**① or regret.

Sandi, I'll get down on my knees if I have to. To let me taste true beauty and love.

Sandi, I love you, and you know that I do. Give me but one day and but one moment in time and 1 will die a happy man...

Well, I better go. It's getting late. I'll see you soon in my dreams, okay?

Bye, Sandi... I'll always love you.

---

① remorse [ri'mɔ:rs] n. 痛悔；自责

美丽语录

I can't give you the whole world. But I will give you the whole of mine.

我不能给你全世界，但是，我的世界，全部给你。

我刚刚结束了与你的通话。我希望在你读到这篇文章的时候，我能在你的身旁，但是实现这个愿望还有很长的路要走……

桑迪，我知道你的心已经属于我，我的心也早已被你俘获。

在我的生命里，你就是我一直等待的那个特别的人，我会对你说出那三个字，并告诉你它们的含义。我明白如果我每天念叨它们，你或许会以为我并不是那个意思。但是请相信我，我所说的每一个字都是我心底的真实表白。

你是我能与之共舞的第一个人。第一个让我有那种感觉的人，第一个让我吐露心底的秘密、而不会感到任何悔恨或遗憾的人。

桑迪，如果需要的话，我心甘情愿跪下双膝。请让我品尝一次真正的甜美和爱情。

桑迪，我爱你，你知道我是真心爱你的。赐予我哪怕一天或一刻的时间，我就会因幸福而死……

就到这里吧，我得走了。现在已经很晚了。我很快就会在梦里遇见你，对吗?

再见，桑迪……我会永远爱你。

苹果皮

◎ Crunchy Betty

"Tell her you got this especially for her," John said to me as he drove, pointing to the basket of fruit wrapped in clear acetate sitting on the back seat. "Remember when you get in, you have to **bow**① to her. Not a half bow but the full bow, the traditional Korean way, with your hands on your forehead." I shifted in the passenger seat uncomfortably. "Then, she's probably going to ask you questions about your **ancestry**②, where you went to school, your goals..."

I was meeting John's mother for the first time this afternoon and he was **fervently**③ coaching me on how to make a good impression. "While she's talking, offer to cut her a piece of fruit from the basket. Cut the fruit in front of her so she can see how well you cut. Get an apple and make sure you peel the skin really thin so that she knows you don't waste food. And make sure you cut it in even slices and lay it down facing the same direction so she knows you can present food in an appetizing manner..." John continued to lecture as I stared blankly out the window.

---

① bow [bəu] v. 鞠躬，欠身
② ancestry ['ænsistri] n.（总称）家族；血统；名门出身
③ fervently ['fə:vəntli] adv. 热烈地，热情地；强烈地

美丽语录

The key for happiness is not to find a perfect person, but find someone and build a perfect relationship with him.

幸福的关键不在于找到一个完美的人，而在于找到一个人，和他一起建立一个完美的关系。

“告诉她，这是你特地为她买的，”约翰一边开车，一边指了指后座上的果篮说道，“记住，一进门时要向她鞠躬。把你的手放在额头上，用韩国传统的全鞠躬方式，而不是半鞠躬。”我产生了一种不自在的感觉，在座位上挪了一下身体。“然后，她可能会问你的家族情况，你所读的学校，你今后的目标……”

今天下午，我第一次去拜访约翰的母亲，为了给他的母亲留下一个好印象，他正在热心地教我怎么做。“当她说话的时候，你主动从果篮里拿一个水果削给她吃。在她的面前削，好让她能看见你削水果的水平。从果篮中拿一个苹果，要把皮削得很薄，让她知道你不会浪费粮食。然后，一定要把苹果切成厚度均匀的片，顺着同一个方向放在盘中，这样她就会知道你是一个注重食物美观的人。”约翰继续侃侃而谈，我漠然地看着窗外。

I had just started dating John, a Korean international student who had been in the States for about 3 years now. I was born in Korea, but I moved to the United States when I was five years old. I know how to speak, read, and write Korean and I thought I had learned enough from my family and watched enough TV programs to know about Korean customs. I guess I was wrong, John and I had our differences. He didn't speak perfect English, but I figured it was okay because I didn't speak perfect Korean either.

But 1ittle problems between our differing cultures surfaced as we continued to date. When we went out to eat, I noticed he'd have trouble reading the menus. When he registered for a class, he scheduled it with my free time so that he had someone to talk for him, like a translator. I accepted the fact that he couldn't speak perfect English, but what was really frustrating was that he wasn't willing to try. It may have been his male pride, but I think he was more embarrassed about the puzzled looks people would give him when he talked.

There would be times when he wouldn't talk single word for hours. It was hard for him to blend in with my Asian-American friends. Once, I and my friends were **reminiscing**[①] about the 80's, things like Michael Jackson, Madonna, teased hair and those awful UMEN cardigans. But while we were laughing away, talking about old times, John just sat there uncomfortably with half a grin on his face. I tried to include him in on our conversations by explaining what we were talking about, but by the look on his face I could tell I wasn't very successful.

One night John came over to my house to pick me up for dinner. My brother's friend Chris was over and they were talking in the living room. Chris said to my brother jokingly, "Man... You're so bad... You're a big pimp." John

① reminisce [,remi'nis] v. 追忆；回想

约翰是一个韩国留学生，他来美国3年了，我与他才刚刚开始约会。我在韩国出生，然而5岁时就移民到了美国。我会说、能读、能写朝鲜语，我自认为通过家庭的熏陶和观看电视节目，已经了解了足够多的韩国风俗文化。不过，看看我和约翰之间的差异，我觉得自己错了。约翰的英语说得不是很熟练，但是我认为还算可以，因为我的朝鲜语说得也不地道。

但是，随着我们约会的次数越来越多，我们之间由于文化差异，逐渐暴露出了一些小问题。我们出去吃饭的时候，我发现他不太能看懂菜单。为了在上课时能让我像翻译一样帮他讲解，他注册课程还专门挑选了我有空闲时间的时候。我愿意接受他英语不好的事实，然而，真正令我感到沮丧的，是他根本不愿意尝试着去说。这可能是男人的自尊心在作怪，不过我认为，他是害怕自己跟别人讲话时，看到别人迷惑不解的样子会更尴尬。

有时候，接连好几个小时，他一个字也不愿意说，很难与我的亚裔美国朋友相处。有一次，我和朋友们回忆起80年代的岁月，像迈克尔·杰克逊、麦当娜、奇异的发型和那些不好看的优盟牌开襟羊毛衫。然而，当我们开怀大笑、畅谈往事时，约翰一脸似笑非笑的样子，不自在地坐在那里。我向他解释我们谈话的内容，努力让他加入我们。然而，从他脸上的表情可以看出，我的努力无动于衷。

一天晚上，约翰到我家接我一起去吃晚餐，正好碰上我弟弟和他朋友克里斯在客厅里聊天。克里斯跟我弟弟开玩笑说："你这个家伙……你真是太坏了……你这个老皮条客。"约翰无意中听到了，试图为我弟弟辩解，便

overheard and replied in his most perfect English, trying to be protective of my brother, "No, he isn't bad, he's actually a good boy. And he is definitely not a playboy." My brother and Chris stared at John in disbelief. Chris was so shocked he apologized to my brother for offending him. As for John, I knew he felt proud for sticking up for my brother. I know he meant well. But he just didn't understand the language.

There were little things that I eventually became accustomed to. For instance, John and I always had to watch TV with the caption turned on and I had to be careful not to use any slang that he wasn't familiar with. I had to speak slower. I always had to explain why we did certain things here, versus how they did them in Korea. I had to constantly recap the stories of the movies we just saw. But the toughest obstacle was trying to describe our feelings or thoughts to each other, trying to learn about our different worlds with our limited vocabularies.

Don't get me wrong. I had a great time learning and experiencing new things with him. We were exposed to different worlds and we taught each other how to cope, accept, and learn in different perspectives. In fact, many couples I know have had successful intercultural relationships. But my relationship made me realize how little cultural differences can make a big difference.

I found that I had a lot more to learn and get accustomed to than I expected. I suppose a successful intercultural relationship depends on how accepting one is to the other's differences and how well a person can adapt to new ideas, thoughts, and lifestyles. Anyway, these relationships can be challenging. As you may have guessed, I'm not with John any more. Meeting his Mom went fine, but I have a feeling I cut the apple skin too thick.

用他说得最好的英语句子解释道："不，他一点都不坏，他是个好男孩，他也绝不是一个花花公子。"我的弟弟和克里斯都难以置信地盯着约翰看，他们简直不敢相信自己的耳朵。克里斯被吓了一跳，赶忙为刚才那个玩笑向我弟弟道歉。我知道，约翰一定为维护我弟弟的尊严而感到自豪。我知道他是好意，他只是不懂语言。

对于生活上的一些小事，我终于习惯了。比如，我和约翰看电视的时候总是打开字幕，我说话的时候尽量避免使用俚语，放慢语速；我总是要向他解释，为什么在这儿要这样做事情，就像他在韩国一样；我还要不断地重述刚刚看过的电影情节。然而，最大的障碍是相互交流彼此的感情和想法，我们只能用有限的词汇了解彼此不同的世界。

不要误解我的意思。与他一起学习和体验新事物的那段日子，我觉得非常快乐。我们生活在不同的世界里，我们教会彼此如何从不同的角度应对、接受和学习。事实上，很多跨文化婚姻中的夫妇生活得都很幸福。然而，我们之间的关系让我体会到了一点，即使是很细微的文化差异，也会让我们产生很大的分歧。

我发现，要学习和适应的事情远远超过了我的想象。我想，如何接受彼此的差异，如何适应新的观念、思想和生活方式，决定着一段跨文化恋情是否能够成功。无论如何，这种跨文化的恋情颇具挑战性。正如你可能猜想到的结局一样，现在，我与约翰已经分手了。对于那次拜访，尽管我觉得自己把苹果皮削得太厚了，但我们相处得还不错。

The Love in Summer

夏日情愫

◎ John Riggio

Buntgh. Bungh. Chh. Bungh-Bungh-Bungh.

Stand by me. This song tells of a time when a summer love that was so sweet that I can taste it even now. It was a time when I anxiously and desperately **yearned for**[①] a girl's touch knowing that touch would immediately melt me like ice in a heat wave.

The voice of Ben E. King still haunts my mind. When the night came that summer I was poised for romance and passion. I wanted to experience that loving feeling that I had heard so much about from the radio and friends. I wanted to be close to a girl. But, not just any girl. The girl I wanted feels like I had just sipped hot chocolate and relaxed all over. Nut brown with black glittering eyes.

And the land is dark and the moon is the only light we'll see. Those words made me feel like I was racing towards the girl. There I would sweep her off her feet with sheer **adoration**[②] and unbridled love. No, I won't be afraid. Just as long as you stand by me. That said it all for me. With her by my side, the world would be my toy.

---

① yearn for 思念；渴望；向往

② adoration [,ædə'reiʃən] n. 崇拜，敬爱；倾慕

美丽语录

Happiness is always knocking on your door and you just gotta let it in.

幸福总会敲响你的门，你只需开门让它进来。

嘭嘭嚓，嘭嘭嘭。

在我的身旁，这首歌倾诉着一段夏日恋情，它是如此甜蜜，以至于现在我还能够回味。这是我极切渴望一个女孩触摸的时期，我相信那个触摸必定会让我似热浪中的冰一样融化。

本·E. 金的声音依然萦绕在我的脑中。在那个夏夜到来之时，为了浪漫和激情，我做好了准备。我盼望着经历多次从广播和朋友那里听来的那种爱的感受。我想接近一个女孩，但是，并非哪个女孩都可以。我想要的那个女孩，她要能让我感觉像刚喝了巧克力热饮那样浑身放松，她要有一双乌黑发亮的栗色眼睛。

四周漆黑一片，月光是我们唯一看到的光亮。那些歌词令我感到自己正朝着那个女孩飞快驶去。我带着纯粹的爱慕和疯狂的爱恋将她一把抱起。不，我不会害怕。只要有你在我的身旁，这已经说出了我的心里话。有她在身旁，世界都能被我征服。

I lived a full life in my mind where she was Queen and I was King. If the sky, that we look upon, should tumble and fall, and the mountains should crumble to the sea. No I won't, I won't cry. No, I won't shed a tear, just as long as you stand, stand by me. I need no other strength than those words.

I would picture myself holding her in my arms, protecting her from the world, planting my love in her heart, but in a reality I knew there was little chance of that ever happening.

But, there was something about that summer than turned a shy boy into a young man. Looking back, I have no idea what it was. Maybe, Ben E. King's voice spurred my maturity. Ben E. King caught the romantic soul of a boy like myself.

And then to my surprise, it happened suddenly. We were standing on her porch looking into the night embraced by the **mellow**[①] voice of Ben E. King coming from the radio. I touched her arm turning her towards me. I think that in that moment she knew what was going to happen.

I leaned forward and I kissed her. I kissed her long, deep and passionately. I kissed her like a man. When it ended, I looked into her eyes. She knew she had been kissed by me.

She seemed as if she were in shock for a moment. So I kissed her again. This time, I kissed her with all the emotion that had been building in me for two full years. We never kissed liked that again. In fact, we never kissed again.

She moved away that summer. But when I hear that—Bungh. Bungh. Chh. Bungh-Bungh-Bungh—I think of her. Sweeter than wine, softer than a summer night.

---

① mellow ['meləu] adj. 圆润的，柔美的

我在思想里过着一种富足的生活。在那里，她是王后，而我是国王。如果我们抬头仰望的天空坍塌，高山化为一片汪洋。不，我不会痛哭流涕。我绝不会流下一滴眼泪，你只需，只需站在我的身旁。除了那些话语，我不需要任何其他力量。

我在想象中拥她入怀，让她不受世界的伤害，在她的心中根植我的爱。然而我知道，这在现实生活中出现的可能性微乎其微。

但是，在那个夏日，某样东西让一个害羞的男孩转变为一个小伙子。回顾过去，我还是不知道那是什么。或许是本 · E. 金的歌声加速了我的成熟。在那个夏日里，本 · E. 金抓住了像我这般男孩的浪漫情怀。

然而出乎我意料的是，事情发生得如此突然。我们站在她的门廊上，夜空中飘荡着收音机里传来的本 · E. 金甜美的歌声。我拉起她的胳膊，让她面向我。我猜那一刻，她明白将会发生什么。

我俯身向前，吻了她，那是一个长久的、深深的、热烈的吻。我像男子汉一样吻着她。然后，我望着她的双眸。她明白我亲吻了她。

那一刻，她仿佛呆住了。因此，我又一次亲吻了她。这一次，我用尽了积蓄整整两年的所有感情亲吻着她。我们再也没有像那样吻过。实际上，我们再也没有亲吻过。

那个夏天，她搬了家。然而每当我听到嘭嘭嚓、嘭嘭嘭的乐声，就会想到她。甜蜜胜过葡萄美酒，轻柔赛过夏日之夜。

The Paradox of Happiness
幸福的悖论

◎ Dennis Palumbo

What is the definition of "happiness"? Is it material wealth filled with fancy cars, a dream house, **extravagant**[①] furs and jewelry? Or is happiness simply having a roof over your head? Food in the fridge? Having a child? A pet? A swimming pool? A designer Gucci bag? Parents? Grandchildren? Love? Money? The perfect job? Winning the Lottery?

According to the American Heritage Dictionary, "happiness" is derived from the Middle English word hap — meaning "Luck". But does happiness really have anything to do with "luck"? Based on this description, one could assume that if you avoided traffic accident but got fired by coming late to work, you would be filled with "happiness"? Is it luck or what you make of it? Maybe, "happiness" is exactly defined by its indirect alias: happiness—perhaps, happiness is in fact defined by the fortune that we permit to happen.

Do you recall a time—let's say when you were about 5 years old—what defined happiness back then? Was it getting a puppy for Christmas? Or maybe, you were a child of divorce; and all you wanted was for Mom and Dad to get

① extravagant [iks'trævəgənt] adj. 奢侈的，浪费的；过度的

美丽语录

If you're brave enough to say goodbye, life will reward you with a new hello.

只要你勇敢地说出再见，生活一定会赐予你一个新的开始。

“幸福”是什么？幸福是拥有豪华的汽车、梦想的居室、名贵的裘皮和珠宝等物质上的富足吗？或者，幸福其实很简单——有遮风避雨的住所，冰箱里有食物，有孩子、宠物、游泳池、古驰的包，有父母、子孙，有爱情、金钱和理想的工作，彩票中了奖？

在《美国传统字典》中，幸福是源于中古英语“hap”一词——意为“好运”。但幸福真的与“好运”有关联？基于此，可以假设，如果你在一场必死无疑的交通事故中幸免于难，却又因为上班迟到而被解雇，你会感到“幸福”吗？这是好运，还是要看个人如何看待？或许，幸福的定义应该间接从它的词源来看——事实上，幸福或许就是命中注定要发生的事。

你能回忆起你 5 岁时对幸福的理解吗？那时，幸福是从圣诞树上摘下的一只小狗？或者，也许你的爸爸妈妈离婚了，你唯一的愿望就是他们能重归于好？当你渐渐长大，你希望有人会邀请你参加舞会，希望所有的日

back together again? Then as you got older, you were hoping that someone would ask you to the prom that would've made your day, maybe your life for the moment. During college, good grades made you happy, but it was short-lived. Because in the real world, you had to look for a job, and competition was stark. It's an employer's world you thought. But then, you got the perfect job—now you could be happy—or could you?

Life requires more than just what we want. Inevitably, one must understand to truly find "happiness," he must make his own happiness "happen". Sounds a bit **redundant**[①], but truthfully, there is no set guidelines that will bring one happiness. There is no "magic wand" we can wave to bring joy into our lives. Human nature thrives on the thrill of the chase. We dream and we hope for the next big break—it is the grand adventure of living.

We are hopeless creatures of comfort. We like having and accumulating things. Whether one admits to it or not, to a certain degree, we all try to keep up with "the Jones". We work so we can pay our rents, mortgages, credit card debts, school loans, car payments...the list goes on and on. And at some point, we realize that aside from having most of what we want, we still aren't happy. Now since we've learned to adapt to new standards which we've created for ourselves, we find that we have less time, less patience, less sleep, which equates to more stress, more worry and more aggravation. So, is happiness honestly just comprised of "things"?

Sometimes, we virtually trade our lives for not only basic necessities, but for excessive items and services as well. We become so **obsessed with**[②] finding

---

① redundant [ri'dʌndənt] adj. 多余的，过剩的；累赘的，冗长的

② （be）obsessed with 着迷，迷恋

子都凝固在那一天、那一刻。上大学期间，好成绩让你快乐无比，但这种幸福感是短暂的。因为在现实世界里，你得找一份工作，而社会竞争也十分激烈。于是，你就会想，这是一个雇主的世界。随后，你找到了一份理想的工作——现在你觉得很幸福，是吗?

生活向我们索要的远比我们想要的多。一个人必须明白，要想真正找到幸福，他就必须让自己幸福。可能听起来有些多余，但确是如此——生活中，没有什么既定准则能带来幸福，也不可能魔杖一挥就得到欢乐。人性在追求幸福的刺激中不断升级、完善。我们梦想着，期望着下一个大的转变——这就是生活中的大冒险。

我们是无助的享乐者，喜欢拥有和积攒东西。不论人们承认与否，在一定程度上，我们都在互相攀比。我们之所以工作，是因为要付房租，偿还抵押贷款，还清信用卡债务、助学贷款、汽车贷款……这些费用接连而至，让我们应接不暇。于是，我们会突然意识到，尽管拥有了想要的一切，我们仍然不幸福。自从适应了自己所创造的新生活标准，我们的时间少了，耐性没了，睡眠少了，但压力大了，焦虑多了，脾气也暴躁了。所以说，幸福真的是由“物质”组成的吗?

有时，我们不仅用生命交换生活必需品，还用生命交换多余的物质享

happiness, that we lose sight of the fact that happiness is within—always. Certainly you've heard of individuals trying to "find themselves", or "rediscover themselves". The reason they are attempting these innovative approaches is because they are seeking inner happiness. But the point has been missed: Happiness is already there.

Disappointments and tragedies in life will come and go, but happiness never leaves you. The human's capacity to be resilient to trials is unfathomable. We can lose our jobs, but be grateful for our spouses. We can lose our homes to nature, but be thankful to alive.

Happiness is a perception of each individual. We are instinctively compelled to find fault in our lives. By human nature, we begin our "fault-find-ing" mission the moment we're capable of free-thinking. It is then, that we lose sense of self-worth and the bigger picture of vitality altogether. Stuck in the patterns of the happiness paradox, we simply cannot find where our happiness has gone.

It's not a matter of bargaining, it's not an issue of money or fame—instead, happiness is what you resolve to accept. If we live through optimistic hope; if we dare to dream; if we empower ourselves to fully live; then we have regained our sense of happiness. There is no in between. There is no other replacement. We only have one physical life to live—we have no choice but to make the most of it.

受和服务。我们变得如此痴迷于追求幸福，却忽略了一个事实——幸福一直就在我们心中。当然，你一定听过有些人在苦苦“寻找自我”或“重新发现自我”。他们创新尝试的理由只不过是为了找寻心灵深处的幸福。但他们忽略了一点：幸福早已在心中了。

失望和悲伤在生命中交替轮回，但幸福从不会舍你而去。人类对困难的适应能力无可限量。我们可以失去工作，但会为拥有爱人而感恩不已；我们可以流离失所，但会为活着而心存感激。

幸福是个人的一种感知。我们本能地受限于外界，找寻着生活的瑕疵。出于人的天性，我们从有能力自由思考的那一刻起，就开始对生活吹毛求疵。也就在那时，我们失去了对自我价值的认知，也失去了生命的活力，陷于幸福的矛盾中，找不到幸福的方向。

幸福是你决定去接受的东西，没有任何商量的余地，它于金钱或名誉毫无瓜葛。只要我们活在乐观希望之中，敢于大胆梦想，活得充实；那么，我们就会重新拥有幸福的感觉。那种感觉并非悬于幸于不幸之间的真空地带，也无任何替代品。我们只能活一次——除了好好活着，我们别无选择。

阅读小课堂

10 Wise Lessons: What I Wish I Knew When I Was Younger

十句箴言：年轻的时候懂这些就好了

◎ Rishi Sankar

1. Don't worry about what other people think of you.

I used to worry too much what others thought of me, of my decisions and of my actions. Eventually, I came to realize that if you're wasting too much time seeking validation, respect or approval from others, then you won't have time to accomplish all that you desire. Everyone has an opinion, but in reality other's opinions of you are based more on their history and perceptions than anything you're actually doing.

2. Today is what't important.

Enjoy every moment of today, because you are not guaranteed a tomorrow. Don't put off your dreams. Don't wait to do, try, enjoy all of those "someday" items. If it's important to you, then do it today. Pay attention to what is happening now, to the people around you, to the task at hand and to all of the choices you

1. 走自己的路，让别人去说吧。

我总是太担心别人怎么想我，怎么看待我的决定和行为。后来，我意识到，如果你把时间浪费在寻求别人的认可、尊重和支持上，那你就根本无暇做你自己想做的事。每个人都有自己的看法，但实际上，其他人对你的看法更多基于他们自身的历史和认知，而并不是你实际在做的事情。

2. 活在当下。

享受今天的每一刻，因为你不能保证明天就一定会到来。不要拖延你的梦想，别等到“有朝一日”再去做，去尝试，去享受。如果真的很重要，那今天就做。关注正在发生的事情，身边的人，手头上的工作，关注今天做出的选择，无论大小。

make today, big and small.

3. Let it go.

What happened yesterday is over. Those unmet expectations, difficult situations, failures and conflicts are in the past. You can't change it, so let it go. Don't waste your energy dwelling on anger, resentment or disappointment. It only keeps you stuck in the past and holds you back from moving forward in your life.

4. It's called work for a reason.

Success at anything takes work. When you hear about an overnight success story, don't forget about all of the work that came before. You may have to do work you do not enjoy and trudge through the trenches of planning, building, refining, moving up, out, over and redefining before you get to the place where success clicks. Keep going.

5. Believe in yourself.

You are your own worst critic, and so can you be your own best supporter. If you do not have confidence in your own value, abilities and contribution, then nobody else will either. You must have faith in your intrinsic worth. We each have something to offer that is necessary and valuable, though we may not know what that something is.

6. Don't burn your bridges.

You never know when a former boss, colleague, business partner or

3. 学会放手。

昨日的一切让它过去。那些没有实现的期待，那些艰难困苦、失败和冲突都已成为过去。你无力改变，所以干脆放手。别把精力浪费在生气、怨恨和失望这些负面情绪上，这些只会让你沉湎过去，让你停在原地。

4. 付出总会有回报。

任何成功都需要付出劳动。你所听到的那些一夜成名的故事，别忘了背后付出的所有劳动和汗水。你可能得做不喜欢的工作，需要在计划、构建、修改、实施、再修改这一系列琐碎的过程中长途跋涉，艰难前行，直到有一天成功破天而降。继续前进。

5. 相信自己。

你是自己最尖刻的批评家，也可以成为自己最大的支持者。假如你对自己的价值、能力和贡献都没有信心，那么其他人更不会相信你。你必须相信自己的内在价值。我们每个人身上都有有价值的东西可以给予，可能我们自己都不知道。

6. 不要自断后路。

你永远都不知道，你的前老板、同事、生意伙伴或熟人说不定哪天会派上用场。好聚好散，和他们保持良好的关系，也别在背后造谣生事。学

acquaintance may come in handy. Try to part on good terms, stay on good terms and never gossip about former connections. Be respectful and open to possibilities. Maintain and foster connections on all levels. Connect others and offer your help to those you know. A wide pool of friends, peers and connections of all kinds will provide a wealthy resource of ideas and support as you go forward in life.

7. Money is not the most important thing.

Money is important. We all have bills to pay, I understand that completely. But in the end, money is not the end goal. Satisfaction in a job well done, contributing to something worthwhile and finding something you enjoy doing are more motivating goals and certainly lend themselves to a happier and less stressful life. Money does not equate to happiness. Money is simply a currency that allows you to eat, dress and live. It is not a magic wand.

8. Don't be afraid to stand up and stand out.

Take a stand. Speak up. Stand out from the crowd. If something is important to you, then stand up for it... Never compromise your integrity. If it's not right, say so. Be quirky, be different, be yourself. Don't worry so much about conforming to society's standards or whatever passes for the norm. While I do think it reasonable to be clean, respectful and considerate, I think we place too much emphasis on fitting in and being "appropriate". This is not your grandmother's world. Don't be afraid to be yourself.

会尊重别人，可能无处不在。保持和维护各级关系网，常和别人联络，尽可能多伸出援手。交友广阔，朋友、同事和其他各种关系人脉会为你未来的生活提供丰富的创意资源和支持。

7. 金钱并不至上。

钱很重要，我们都有账单要付，我完全能理解。但最终你会发现，金钱并不是终极目标。圆满完成工作的满足感，为一些有价值的事情作贡献，还有找到自己爱做的事，这些目标会让你更加有动力，也会为你带来更幸福更轻松的生活。金钱不等于幸福。钱只是一种货币，让我们吃、穿、生活，它并不是神奇的魔杖。

8. 勇敢地站起来，让自己脱颖而出。

站起来，说出来，让自己从人群中脱颖而出。如果有样东西对你很重要，那就站起来……不要放弃你的正直。如果你觉得不对，就说出来。特立独行，与众不同，做自己就好。别事事担心要循规蹈矩，要遵循社会的标准和准则。衣着整洁、尊重有礼、体贴周到，这样就可以了，不用过多强调融入他人和举止得体。如今不是你祖母的老世界，别害怕做你自己。

9. It's not a race.

We have so much to do, so much to accomplish and it feels as though we have to be in a hurry to get there. It is likely that you will live upwards of 80 years. That is plenty of time to fit a whole host of wonderful endeavors into your life. You do not have to do it all at once. In fact, if you try to do it all at once you will, at best not have time to enjoy it and at worst burn out and damage your health and relationships. Slow down and take one thing at a time, one day at a time.

10. Look for the good in everything.

Stay positive. Look for the good in people. Celebrate the happy moments, big and small. Give helpful encouragement rather than negative criticism. If you view the world around you and life's challenges through the lens of goodness, then you will find life much more enjoyable.

Life is serious—and sometimes awful—but you can still be upbeat and hopeful. Otherwise, what's the point?

9. 生活不是竞赛。

我们有这么多事要做，这么多梦想要实现，所以我们时刻匆忙行走，赶来赶去。也许我们可能会活到 80 岁。我们有大量的时间可以努力。不用急着一次干完所有事情。事实上，如果你想要一次做好所有，最好的结果是你没享受过程，最坏的结果是你消耗了健康，毁掉了感情。慢慢来，一次干一件事情，日子一天一天地过。

10. 凡事看到好的一面。

保持积极向上。要看到别人的优点，庆祝生活中大大小小的快乐瞬间。多给别人暖心的鼓励，而不是负面的批评。如果你用善意的视角看待周围的世界和生活的挑战，你会发现生活会更美好。

生活是严肃的——有时会很糟糕——但你依然可以乐观向上、充满希望。否则，人生又有什么意义呢?

Chapter 2

梦想的袅袅回音

Your dream is not what you find in your sleep but what makes you not sleep.

所谓梦想，不是你睡觉时梦到了什么，而是想到了什么令你激动得没法睡觉。

An Unlikely Hero
另类英雄

◎ Tony Luna

When Dr. Gullickson was assigning project mates for his introduction to experimental psychology class, I secretly hoped he would pair me with a cute coed or at least a classmate I could have some fun with. Above all, I hoped he wouldn't assign me to work with the intense, fiercely competitive, **singularly**[①] serious fellow who always wore dark clothes and apparently had a personality to match. As fate would have it, Dr. Gullickson very deliberately matched everyone in class and announced that I would be working with the one person in class I wanted to avoid.

I went up to my new lab mate and introduced myself. He looked at me as though I weren't there. I felt he treated me as though I would hold him back and probably cause his grade-point average to take a **nosedive**[②]. He wasn't outright mean or abusive. He just gave me the impression he could do whatever project we dreamed up better if he did it alone. He was a loner, and I could only impede his research. He had important things to do, and I was going to be something of

① singularly ['siŋgjuləli] adv. 非常地，格外地；异常地

② nosedive ['nəuzdaiv] n. 猛跌；低落；情况突然变坏

美丽语录

When someone allows you to bear his burdens, you have found deep friendship.

如果有人愿意让你替他承担一些事情，你已经找到了深厚的友谊。

当格利克森博士正在为实验心理学课分配研究小组时，我暗暗地祈祷他能把我与一个可爱的女生，至少是一个志趣相投的同学分在一组。总而言之，我希望他不要让我与一个竞争意识强烈、异常严肃的家伙做搭档，这种人总爱穿深色的衣服，而且还有着十足的个性。命运弄人，格利克森博士在一番深思熟虑后，向每个人宣布了结果，而我与一个我最想躲避的人成为一组。

我走到自己的实验搭档面前，做了自我介绍。他看着我，好像我并不存在似的。我感觉到，他似乎认为我会阻碍他进步，并且可能导致他的平均成绩直线下降。他并没表现恶意，只是给了我这样的印象，无论什么实验，如果他独自去做就会做得更好。他完全能独立完成任务，他有重要的事情要做，而我只会妨碍他的研究，只能成为他不得不花时间和精力应付

an annoyance he'd have to deal with.

Needless to say, I didn't look forward to an entire semester of being brushed off, but I tried to make the best of it and didn't say anything, lest I make things worse.

The project required each lab team to develop a hypothesis, set up an experiment to test the hypothesis, run the tests, do the statistical analysis and present the findings. Whatever grade the team received would be shared by both students. When my lab mate and I met to discuss our project, I was uneasy. Here was this challenging student who had a reputation for single-mindedness and good grades—the exact opposite of me. 1 was outmatched. I actually wanted to drop the class at one point, but stopped short because I didn't want to give him the satisfaction of my chickening out. I asked my friends at work what I should do, and the overall response was to stick it out no matter what.

After lengthy discussions, we somehow agreed to do a study on the tactile-kinesthetic perception of space. I wasn't sure what it meant, but at least we had a topic. We started to meet regularly to formulate our plans, and every time I felt the project was more his than mine. The more we met, the more I resented his intelligence and his ability to cut through to the core issues. And I was aware he was much more advanced than I. He knew technical things and approached every detail with great singularity of purpose.

I, on the other hand, must have seemed naive, with little to offer. At one point I summoned up my courage and asked him why he seemed so uptight and serious. To my surprise, he replied that he didn't have time for small talk or petty people and things that would waste his time. He even went on to say that he didn't have many friends because most so-called friends were just a distraction.

的麻烦。

当然，我可不想把整个学期都荒废掉，为了避免事情变得更糟，我什么也没说，只是尽最大的努力做好实验。

根据计划，每个实验小组要提出假设、制定实验检验假设、进行统计学分析、介绍研究结果。小组取得的成绩就是每个小组成员的成绩。我每次都忐忑不安地与同伴讨论实验的问题。他在这里是出了名的专注和优秀，他是一个勇于挑战的人——而我与他完全相反。事实上，我心里曾经有过放弃的念头，然而，我不想被他看扁，所以很快放弃了这种想法。我向那些忙于工作的朋友请教我该怎么做，他们的回答全部是，无论发生什么，坚持到底。

经过长时间的讨论后，我们终于达成一致，决定做一项关于空间触觉和动觉感知的研究。我并不明白这是一项什么研究，但至少我们确定了一个题目。为了制定计划，我们定期碰面，每次讨论决定之后，我都觉得是他制定了计划。我们碰面的次数越多，我就越是痛恨他的才智和直击问题核心的能力。我逐渐意识到，他的水平比我高很多。他了解技术，并且能带着明确的目标去处理每一个细节问题。

另一方面，我能提出的建议微乎其微，有时看起来的确天真。有一次，我鼓起勇气问他，他为什么看起来那么紧张严肃。令我吃惊的是，他回答我说他没时间闲聊，对他来说，无聊的人和事只是浪费时间。他甚至还说，他没有很多朋友，因为那些所谓的朋友只会令人分心。不过，他补充道，

But, he added, when he did choose someone to be his friend, thcy would be a friend for life. I was floored by his cold and cynical response. Right then and there, I realized the end of the semester couldn't come soon enough.

As the semester wore on, we tried to fashion a simple yet elegant experiment. Part of our job was to select students who had volunteered to be subjects for our project. I decided to devote myself to the task of working with the subjects, while he developed the scientific model. I put in my two cents' worth whenever I could, but I still felt he was the driving force.

Then one day I got word that he was in hospital. Apparently, he had been admitted for a hemorrhaging ulcer. The stress of getting the best grades, holding down a job and helping his girlfriend through the medical crisis she was going through had taken its toll on him.

When I visited him in the hospital, I noticed for the first time a sense of vulnerability on the face of my stoic lab mate. I knew that he was aware that I could blow the experiment, and our shared grade would shatter his lofty G. P. A. and possibly derail his chances for graduate school. I assured him I would not let him down and he should only **concentrate on**[①] getting better. I would do my best. We both knew I'd have to do better than my best.

I had a formidable task ahead of me. I was in over my head, running the statistical data. I poured more time and energy into that project than I had ever done on any assignment in my life. I was not going to let him see me fail and have it reflect on him. I was working the graveyard shift at my job, so I used whatever quiet time from midnight to 6:00 A. M. to work on the project. The work consumed me. There was a sense of challenge that completely overtook

---

① concentrate on 集中精力，一心一意

一旦他选择某人作为自己的朋友，他就会把他们当作一生的朋友。他那冷淡和玩世不恭的态度让我十分震惊。就在那时，我恨不得这个学期马上结束。

时光荏苒，我们尝试设计了一个操作简单且非常出色的实验。挑选自愿做实验对象的学生成了我们的一部分工作，我决定致力于招募研究对象，而他负责阐述科学方法。我抓住一切可能的机会陈述自己的意见，然而，我仍然有一种感觉：他才是整个实验的驱动力。

后来有一天，我得知他生病住进了医院。很显然，他是因为出血性溃疡才住院的。他想取得最好的成绩，想找一份工作，想帮助生病的女朋友度过危险期，这些压力把他压垮了。

当我到医院探望他时，我第一次注意到，这个坚忍克己的实验伙伴的脸上有了一种脆弱的表情。我知道，他是担心我会把实验搞砸，担心他的总平均成绩被小组实验成绩毁掉，甚至会突然失去进研究院的机会。我向他保证，我一定会付出最大的努力不让他失望，让他一心一意恢复健康。我们都清楚，我必须比最好做得还要好。

任务十分艰巨。我埋头整理统计数据，这些资料已经超出了我的理解范围。我有生以来所做的任何作业，都不曾付出过这么多的时间和精力。我不能让他看到我失败，不愿意因为我而影响他的成绩。为了能安静地做研究，我把工作时间调整到夜里，从午夜一直干到凌晨六点。我被工作吸引住了，感觉自己全身心地投入到了一场挑战之中。但问题仍然存在，我

me. The question remained: Was I up to it?

Eventually, the semester came to a close, and each team had to present its findings in front of the assembled class. When it was our turn, I did my level best to present his scientific methodology with my showmanship. To my amazement, we were awarded an A!

When I told my lab mate about our shared triumph, he smiled and thanked me for carrying on. Something connected then. Something special. It had to do with trust and the exhilaration of sharing a cornmon prize.

We have stayed close throughout the years. He went on to achieve a doctorate. He also went on to marry his college girlfriend.

I learned more than statistical analysis and experimental procedures that semester. My life has been enhanced by our encounter and challenged by this man, who became my unlikely hero.

And in the end, he was right: we have become friends for life.

能解决吗?

这个学期即将结束的时候，各个小组终于要在所有小组前陈述自己的研究成果了。轮到我们时，我用自己最好的表演技巧阐述了他的科学方法，我竭尽了全力。令我异常惊喜的是，我们得了“A”！

当我告诉我的实验伙伴，我们的共同努力取得了成功时，他笑了笑，感谢我完成了实验。那一刻，某些特别的东西将我们联系在了一起。这些特别的东西，与信任有关，与分享获奖的喜悦有关。

这些年来，我们仍然保持着密切的关系。他已经获得了博士学位，也与他的大学女友建立了家庭。

那个学期，我学到了更多的东西，而不仅仅是统计学分析和实验过程。他是我生活中的另类英雄，我的生活因他而面临挑战，因他而变得广阔。

事实证明，他说得没错：我们成了一生的朋友。

Don't Work for Money
不做有才华的穷人

© Patty Hansen

The world is filled with smart, talented, educated and gifted people. We meet them every day. A few days ago, my car was not running well. I pulled it into a garage, and the young **mechanic**① had it fixed in just a few minutes. He knew what was wrong by simply listening to the engine. I was amazed. The sad truth is, great talent is not enough.

I am constantly shocked at how little talented people earn. I heard the other day that less than 5 percent of Americans earn more than $100,000 a year. A business consultant who specializes in the medical trade was telling me how many doctors, dentists and chiropractors struggle financially. All this time, I thought that when they graduated, the dollars would **pour in**②. It was this business consultant who gave me the phrase, "They are one skill away from great wealth." What this phrase means is that most people need only to learn and master one more skill and their income would jump exponentially. I have mentioned before that financial intelligence is a synergy of accounting, investing,

① mechanic [mi'kælik] n. 机械工，技工，修理工

② pour in 蜂拥而来

美丽语录

Don't say that opportunities never come. It came but you just don't willing to give up the things you own.

不要说机会从来没有出现，它曾经出现过，只是你舍不得放下自己拥有的东西。

这个世界随处可见精明能干、才华横溢、学富五车和极具天赋的人。我们每天都能见到他们。几天前，我的车运转不良了。我把它送到一个修车厂，一个年轻的机械工只花了几分钟就把它修好了。他只是听了听发动机的声音就知道毛病出在哪儿，这让我惊叹不已。然而遗憾的是，空有一身才华是不够的。

才华横溢的人却收入甚微，这常常让我感到吃惊。前几天我听说，只有不到5%的美国人年收入在10万美元以上。一个精通药品贸易的商业顾问曾告诉我，有很多医生、牙医和按摩师正面临着经济困难。以前，我们总以为他们一毕业，滚滚而来的便是万贯财富。这位商业顾问还告诉我一句话："想要财源滚滚，他们还差一项技能。"这句话的意思就是：大多数人还需要学习和掌握一项技能，这样他们的收入才会突飞猛涨。我曾提到过，财商是会计、投资、市场营销和法律的综合体。将上面这四种专业技

marketing and law. Combine those four technical skills and making money with money is easier. When it comes to money, the only skill most people know is to work hard.

When I graduated from the U.S. Merchant Marine Academy in 1969, my educated dad was happy. Standard Oil of California had hired me for its oil-tanker fleet. I had a great career ahead of me, yet I resigned after six months with the company and joined the Marine Corps to learn how to fly. My educated dad was devastated. Rich dad congratulated me.

Job security meant everything to my educated dad. Learning meant everything to my rich dad. Educated dad thought I went to school to learn to be a ship's officer. Rich dad knew that I went to school to study international trade. So as a student, I made cargo runs, navigating large freighters, oil tankers and passenger ships to the Far East and the South Pacific. While most of my classmates, including Mike, were partying at their fraternity houses, I was studying trade, people and cultures in Japan, Thailand, Singapore, Hong Kong, Vietnam, Korea and the Philippines. I also was partying, but it was not in any frat house. I grew up rapidly.

There is an old cliché that goes, "Job is an **acronym**① for 'Just over Broke'." And unfortunately, I would say that the saying applies to millions of people. Because school does not think financial intelligence is intelligence, most workers "live within their means". They work and they pay the bills. Instead I recommend to young people to seek work for what they will learn, more than what they will earn. Look down the road at what skills they want to acquire before choosing a specific profession and before getting trapped in the

① acronym ['ækrəunim] n. 首字母缩写

能结合起来，那么以钱生钱就更加容易了。一谈到钱，大多数人就只知道埋头苦干这个唯一的技能。

1969 年，我从美国海运学院毕业。我那知识渊博的爸爸高兴坏了，因为加州标准石油公司录用了我，我在该公司的油轮队工作。尽管我前程似锦，六个月后我还是离开了这家公司。我加入了海军陆战队，并学习如何飞行。我那学识渊博的爸爸伤透了心，而富爸爸却祝贺了我。

对于学识渊博的爸爸来说，稳定的工作就是一切；而对于富爸爸来说，学习才是一切。学识渊博的爸爸认为我上学是为了成为一位船长；而富爸爸觉得我是为了学习国际贸易。所以，作为一名学生的同时，我还跑过货运，为开往远东和南太平洋的大型货轮、游轮和客轮导航。当我的大部分同班同学，包括迈克，在他们的联谊会会堂开晚会的时候，我正在学习日本、泰国、新加坡、香港、越南、韩国和菲律宾的贸易、人际关系和文化。当然，我也会参加晚会，但我不会参加任何联谊会。就这样，我迅速成长起来了。

有句老话是这么说的："工作 (Job) 就是'比破产强一些'(Just over Broke) 的缩写。"然而真正不幸的是，这句话适用于成千上万的人。因为学校并没有把财商看作是一种才智，大多数工人都是"量入为出"的：上班赚钱还清账单。相反，我建议年轻人找工作时应该考虑能从工作中学到什么，而不是光看能赚到多少钱。在选择特定行业和陷入"老鼠赛跑"(激烈竞争) 之前，好好想想自己想要获得怎样的技能。人们一旦陷入偿还账

"Rat Race". Once people are trapped in the lifelong process of bill paying, they become like those little hamsters running around in those little metal wheels. Their little furry legs are spinning furiously, the wheel is turning furiously, but come tomorrow morning, they'll still be in the same cage: great job.

When I ask the classes I teach, "How many of you can cook a better hamburger than McDonald's?" almost all the students raise their hands. I then ask, "So if most of you can cook a better hamburger, how come McDonald's makes more money than you?" The answer is obvious: McDonald's is excellent at business systems. The reason so many talented people are poor is because they focus on building a better hamburger and know little or nothing about business systems. The world is filled with talented poor people. All too often, they're poor or struggle financially or earn less than they are capable of, not because of what they know but because of what they do not know. They focus on perfecting their skills at building a better hamburger rather than the skills of selling and delivering the hamburger.

单的悲惨命运里，就和那些在小铁轮上不停奔跑转圈的小老鼠一样了。小老鼠的小腿飞快地蹬着，小铁轮也飞快地转着，可是第二天早晨，它们仍旧待在那个老鼠笼里：那就是重要的工作。

当我在自己教课的班级里问道："你们当中有多少人做的汉堡比麦当劳的好吃？"几乎全班的学生都举起手来。于是，我接着问道："如果你们大多数人做的汉堡都比麦当劳的好吃，那为什么麦当劳赚的却比你们多呢？"答案是显而易见的：麦当劳有一套完美的商业运营体系。许多才华横溢的人却很贫穷，原因就是：他们只关心如何做出更好的汉堡，却对商业运营体系一无所知。这个世界到处都是有才华的穷人。在很多情况下，他们贫穷、经济拮据或者收入和才能不相符，不是因为他们已知的东西，而是因为他们未知的东西。他们只注重于提高和完善汉堡的技术，而完全忽略了汉堡的销售和送货技能。

Dreams Are the Stuff Life Is Made of

梦想构造生活

◎ Carroll Carroll

I believe I'm a very lucky man.

My entire life has been lived in the healthy area between too little and too much. I've never experienced financial or emotional insecurity, but everything I have, I've **attained**① by my own work, not through indulgence, inheritance or privilege.

Never having lived by the abuses of any extreme, I've always felt that a workman is worthy of his hire, a merchant entitled to his profit, an artist to his reward.

As a result of all this, my bargaining bump may be a little underdeveloped, so I've never tried to oversell myself. And though I may work for less than I know I can get, I find that because of this, I'm never so afraid of losing a job that I'm forced to compromise with my principles.

Naturally in a life as mentally, physically, emotionally and financially fortunate as mine has been, a great many people have helped me. A few meant to,

① attain ['ətein] v. 达到，获得，到达

美丽语录

It's not about what you say; it's about what you do.

关键不是你说什么，而是你做什么。

我相信自己是一个幸运的人。

我的整个一生都十分平稳，毫无波澜。我从未经历过经济或情感危机，但我所拥有的一切并不是依靠溺爱、遗产或特权，而是通过自己的努力工作得来的。

在生活中我从不滥走极端，我总觉得工人就应当工作，商人就应当获利，艺术家就应当获取报酬。

正因如此，我讨价还价的能力没有丝毫长进，所以我从不试图过分吹嘘自己。尽管我知道我得到的少于实际应得的，但我仍会继续工作。我发现，这样一来，我从未因害怕失业而做出任何违背原则的事。

的确，像我这种在精神、身体、情感和经济上都如此幸运的人，少不了很多人曾给予的帮助。有些帮助是刻意的，但大多数都是偶然为之。尽

most did so by accident. I still feel I must **reciprocate**[①]. This doesn't mean that I've dedicated my life to my fellow man. I'm not the type. But I do feel I should help those I'm qualified to help, just as I've been helped by others.

What I'm saying now is, I feel, part of that pattern. I think everyone should, for his own sake, try to reduce to six hundred words the beliefs by which he lives—it's not easy—and then compare those beliefs with what he enjoys—not in real estate and money and goods, but in love, health, happiness and laughter.

I don't believe we live our lives and then receive our reward or punishment in some afterlife. The life and the reward... the life and the punishment—these to me are one. This is my religion, coupled with the firm belief that there is a Supreme Being who planned this world and runs it so that "no man is an island entire of himself..." The dishonesty of any one man subverts all honesty. The lack of ethics anywhere adulterates the whole world's ethical content. In these—honesty and ethics—are, I think, the true spiritual values.

I believe the hope for a thoroughly honest and **ethical**[②] society should never be laughed at. The most idealistic dreams have repeatedly forecast the future. Most of the things we think of today as hard, practical and even indispensable were once merely dreams.

So I like to hope that the world need not be a dog-eat-dog jungle. I don't think I'm my brother's keeper. But I do think I'm obliged to be his helper. And that he has the same obligation to me.

In the last analysis, the entire pattern of my life and belief can be found in the words "Do not do unto others that which you would not have others do unto

---

① reciprocate [ri'siprəkeit] v. 交换；报答；互给

② ethical ['eθikəl] adj. 伦理的，道德的

管如此，我仍然觉得应当报答他们。这并不意味着我把我的生命都奉献给了我的同胞们，我也不是那样的人。但我确实觉得应该尽自己所能去帮助他人，就像别人帮助我一样。

我认为，现在所说的这些正是我信仰中的一部分。即使很难，但为了自己，每个人都应将自己的信念缩减到六百字，并与他所享有的东西作比较——不比拥有的房产、金钱和物品，而是比爱、健康、幸福和欢笑。

我不相信，今生的生活方式会在来世遭到报应。生活与奖赏……生活与惩罚——对我而言，是同一回事。这就是我的信仰，与之紧紧相连的，是我坚信上帝创造并操纵着这个世界，使“任何人都不是一座孤岛……”个人的欺诈会破坏所有人的正直。无论何处的道德沦丧了，都会使全世界的道德变质。我认为，只有诚实与道德才拥有真正的精神价值。

我相信，永远不应嘲笑对构建诚实与道德社会的期望。最理想的梦想往往反复预示着未来。如今，我们觉得困难的、实用的、甚至不可或缺的许多东西，曾经也只是梦想。

所以，我希望这个世界不再是弱肉强食的世界。我不认为自己是多管闲事的人。但我觉得自己有义务去帮助他人，就像他人有义务帮助我一样。

you." To say "Do unto others as you would have others do unto you" somehow implies bargaining, an offer of favor for favor. But to restrain from acts which you, yourself, would abhor is an exercise in will power that must raise the level of human relationship.

"What is unpleasant to thyself," says Hillel, "That do not unto thy neighbor. This is the whole law." and he concluded. "All else is exposition."

总而言之，“无论做什么，你希望别人如何待你，就要如何对待别人。”这句话涵盖了我的整个生活与信仰。“要想别人如何待你，你也要如何对待别人”暗示着礼尚往来的交易。然而，不做连自己都厌恶的事则是一种对意志力的磨炼，这也会使人际关系有所改善。

希勒尔说：“己所不欲，勿施于人。这就是全部法则。”他总结道：“余下的所有只是对它的阐述。”

Do You Have Your Wallet
你有钱包吗

◎ Laksman Frank

This is a story about a learning experience that had a big effect on the way that I live my life. The teacher in the story did not scream, assign homework, give me tests or even grade me on my work. I was taught by one of the most effective methods of teaching, one that only people with lots of love can do.

"My wallet! Where is it?" were my first words when I found my wallet was missing. I searched my memory for a few good seconds, then realized that I had left my **precious**① wallet at the library. Not only did I leave it at the library, but I had left it in the library's public restroom! I distinctly remembered seeing it on the shelf as I went to the bathroom.

Because the library was now closed, I had to wait until the next morning to begin my search. When I got there the next day, all I found was a sparkling clean restroom, its counters clean and its floors shiny white. This was the first time I could remember ever hating to see a clean bathroom. As I walked out, I looked at myself in the mirror and shook my head at the forgetful fool in front of me.

Now all I could hope for was that the person who cleaned the restroom had found my wallet. So I politely approached an old lady reading her book at the front desk. I asked her if a wallet had been found in the bathroom yesterday.

---

① precious ['preʃəs] adj. 贵重的；珍爱的

美丽语录

How do you get people to help you? You can't get there alone. People have to help you and I do believe in karma. I believe in paybacks.

怎么才能让别人向你伸出援手？你不能孤军奋战。有人会来帮你，我相信因果报应。我相信回报。

这是一个让我有所收获的故事，它对我的生活方式产生了巨大的影响。在这个故事中，没有老师的厉声尖叫，没有家庭作业，没有考试，甚至没有功课成绩评定。然而，那却是对我来说最有效的教学方法，只有富有爱心的人才能做到。

“我的钱包！在哪儿呢？”当我发现钱包不见了以后，这就是我说的第一句话。我回想了好几秒钟，然后才意识到我把贵重的钱包落在图书馆了，而且是图书馆的公共洗手间！我清楚地记得，我走进洗手间时，还看见它在架子上。

图书馆现在已经闭馆了，我只好等到第二天早晨再去找。第二天一到图书馆，我就看到洗手间里干净整洁，洗手台擦得一尘不染，地板反射出亮光。我仍然记得，那是我第一次讨厌看到洗手间这么干净。我走了出去，看着镜子中的自己，对着面前这个健忘的傻瓜摇了摇头。

现在，我只能寄望于洗手间的清洁工捡到我的钱包了。于是，我向一位坐在前台看书的上了年纪的夫人走去，我表现得很有礼貌。我问她昨天有没有在洗手间捡到了一个钱包。她并没有立即回答我，直到读到一个认

She didn't answer me until she found a good place to pull herself away from her book. Then she peered at me from behind the thick black glasses parked on her nose. Letting out a quiet sigh, she slowly struggled out of her comfortable sitting position. She walked through a door and **vanished**① for a moment. Then she came back to the desk.

"No."

That was that. I quickly thanked her and walked off.

I wondered what I would do if I had found a wallet containing sixty dollars, a phone card and many other irreplaceable personal items. Finally, I painfully accepted the fact that my wallet was gone.

A week later, after I had canceled my bank card and reported my license missing, I received a mysterious package in the mail. Sure enough, it was my wallet! And most amazingly, nothing was missing! But something was different about it. There was a little yellow sheet of paper folded up in one of the wallet pockets that had not been there before. I slowly unfolded the paper. Into my hand fell a little copper **medallion**② of Christ. The letter read something like this:

Always keep this medallion with you, no matter what your religion is, so that the angel that was watching over you last week will always be close.

This person didn't even leave a return address. So I couldn't thank whoever it was. I felt that this was an act of pure kindness that was extremely rare.

From that day on, I promised myself that whenever I am in a situation where I can help others the way that this person helped me, I will follow this example and make them as happy as I was when I opened that package!

① vanished ['væniʃ] v. 突然不见；消逝；绝迹

② medallion [mi'dæljən] n. 奖章

为可以中断的地方。接着，她眯着眼睛，从鼻梁上那副厚厚的黑框眼镜后面凝视着我。她轻轻地叹了一口气，缓缓地从舒服的座椅上挣扎下来，走进一个门后不见了。片刻之后，她又回到了前台。

“没有。”

除此之外，她什么都没说。我迅速地向她道谢，然后就走开了。

如果我捡到了一个钱包，里面装着 60 美元、一张电话卡和许多别人无法使用的私人物品，我也想知道自己会怎么做。我的钱包已经丢了。最终，我不得不痛苦地接受这个事实。

银行卡注销和证件挂失一周后，我收到一个神秘的包裹。我确信，那就是我的钱包！最让人惊讶的是，一样物品也没少！唯一不同的是，我在钱包夹层里发现一张从来没见过的、折叠起来的黄色小纸条。我慢慢地展开纸条，一枚铜质的基督徽章掉落到我手里。纸条上写着：

把这枚徽章永远戴在身上，不管你的宗教信仰是什么。这样，上周守护你的天使将会永远陪伴着你。

这个寄包裹的人甚至没有留下地址。因此，我也不知道应该向谁致谢。我感觉到，这是世界上最珍贵、最纯粹的善良。

从那天起，我向自己发誓，无论何时，只要我能够做到，我都会去帮助别人，就像帮助我的那个人一样。我要把那个人当作榜样，让别人体会到我打开包裹时的那种喜悦！

Everyone Is Important
每个人都重要

© Ron Hubbard

On the first day of the new term in a community primary school in Germany, after guiding the pupils to sing songs, the priest stepped down the platform, sat on a seesaw and asked one child to sit on the other side but he fail to raise the priest up; another child sat on the seesaw and he was in vain too; then the third child sat on and the priest's side was finally raised up. All those present gave warm **applauses**① for that. The priest said with a solemn look, "Every child is important. Because of him, everything will be different."

Everyone is very important. A string of beads, when clustered together, are beads; when scattered, they are just lonely prayers, which are so fainted that God cannot hear.

God let us be born and would give everyone a responsibility to take. Some people are flowers while others are leaves; some people are vines while others tendrils; some people are tea while others wine; some people are jades while others stones; some people are like waterfalls while others brooks.

Some people are destined to be a legend while others ordinary; some

① applause [ə'plɔ:z] n. 鼓掌欢迎，喝彩；称赞

美丽语录

Don't let the noise of others' opinions drowns out your own inner voice, and most important, have the courage to follow your heart and intuition.

不要让别人的看法淹没了自己心底的声音，最重要的是，要有勇气跟随自己的内心与直觉。

德国一所社区小学开学的第一天，神父带领大家唱歌后，走下讲台坐上跷跷板，请一个孩子坐在另一头，但他没能把神父翘起来；再来一个孩子，也没有用；又来了第三个，终于把神父坐的那一头翘起来了。全场响起了热烈的掌声。神父神情严肃地说：“每个孩子都是重要的。因为，有了他，一切都会不同。”

每个人都很重要。一串念珠，串起来是念珠；散开了，就只是一个个孤独的祷告，微弱得无法让神听到。

上帝让我们降生，便会给每个人一份责任。有些人是花，有些人是叶；有些人是藤，有些人是蔓；有些人是茶，有些人是酒；有些人是玉器，有些人是石头；有些人是瀑布，有些人是小溪。

有些人注定是传奇，有些人注定平淡庸常；有些人注定名声大作，有

are destined to be famous while others unknown; some people are destined to possess favorable reputation while others have few visitors and no care for them.

However, everyone is quite important. You may be **humble**① and insignificant but it won't work without you.

You are punctuations among a pile of arrogant words, though tiny and self-abased, you do play a significant role! You can help them to breathe and adjust their tones. You can either carry them through without stopping just like floating clouds and flowing water or make them rise and fall just like clang.

You are a musical note, breathing as **feebly**② as that of tadpoles but you can dance on the musician's fingertip. Nobody can see you because you are invisible, but when you get together with your numerous sisters and you will definitely compose gorgeous melodies to amaze the world.

You are a lonely string of knitting wool but people can knit you into a sweater or scarf with charming and tenderness to protect people against the cold in winter.

You are a lonely footprint but the other different footprints shall overlap with you ceaselessly and make a path to happiness.

You are humble but still can do something noble. You can use your tolerance to put out some indignant fire; you can use a simple philanthropic act to lighten those apathetic hearts; you can turn over the Bible to open windows of love for children.

Everyone is quite important, and is justifiable for being born.

From the very moment you were born, you began to share every ray of

---

① humble ['hʌmbl] adj. 谦逊的；卑微的

② feebly ['fi:bli] adv. 衰弱地；无力地

些人注定默默无声；有些人注定声名显赫，有些人注定无人问津、无人在意。

然而，每个人都很重要。你可以卑微，可以渺小，但缺少了你，一样也不可以。

你是标点，在一大堆傲慢的文字里面，渺小而自卑，但作用却举足轻重！你可以帮助它们呼吸，调节它们的语气。或让它们一气呵成，如行云流水；或让它们抑扬顿挫，如铿锵之音。

你是一个音符，蝌蚪一般呼吸微弱，但却在音乐家的指尖上舞蹈。你是无形的，别人看不到你，但当你和众多姐妹在一起时，就会谱写出最美妙的旋律，让世界惊艳！

你是一根孤单的毛线，但人们可以将你编织成毛衣或围巾，妩媚而温情，为人们在冬天里御寒。

你是一个寂寞的脚印，但另一些不同的脚印会不停地与你重叠，踩出一条通往幸福的路。

你是谦卑的，但依然可以去做高尚的事。你可以用你的宽容，去熄灭一些愤怒的火；你可以用一个简单的善举，来点燃那些冷漠的心；你可以翻开《圣经》，为孩子们敞开一扇扇爱的窗口，让他们梦想着去做一个帮助他人的天使。

每个人都很重要，诞生便有它的理由。

从诞生的那一刻起，你开始分享世界的每一缕阳光，感恩世界的每一

sunshine in the world and feel grateful for every drop of raindrop in the word, therefore it is imperative for you undertake the responsibility of decorating the world: you are a tree and numerous "you" can grow into a forest; you are a star and numerous "you" can form the Milky Way; you are a piece of brick and numerous "you" can build the mansions; you are a flower and numerous "you" can became a garden; you are a drop of water and numerous "you" can become the ocean.

God also plays the seesaw and looks at the people on the other side, who get on one by one and raise him up gradually.

"Everyone is quite important, and has his own position... " looking at the people in every corner of the world, God said in relief, with a delighted smile on his exhausted face.

滴雨水，也必然要承担起装扮世界的责任：你是一棵树，众多的“你”便长成了森林；你是一颗星，众多的“你”便聚成了星河；你是一块砖，众多的“你”便砌成了大厦；你是一朵花，众多的“你”便开成了花园；你是一滴水，众多的“你”便汇成了海洋。

上帝也坐上跷跷板，看另一头的人，一个个坐上来，渐渐把他跷起来。

“每个人都很重要，每个人都有属于自己的位置……”望着世界每个角落的人，上帝如释重负地说，疲惫的脸上露出欣慰的笑容。

Life Is a Test
生活是一场测试

◎ Ashley Goodale

One of my favorite posters says, "Life is a test. It is only a test. Had this been a real life you would have been instructed where to go and what to do." Whenever I think of this humorous bit of wisdom, it reminds me not to take my life so seriously.

When you look at life and its many challenges as a test, or series of test, you begin to see each issue you face as an opportunity to grow, a chance to discover more about life. Whether you are being **bombarded**① with problems, responsibilities, even **insurmountable**② difficulties, when look at as a test, you always have a chance to succeed, in the sense of rising above that which is challenging you. If, on the other hand, you see each new issue you face as a serious battle that must be won in order to survive, you're probably in for a very rocky journey. The only time you are likely to be happy is when everything is working out just right. And we all know how often that happens.

As an experiment, see if you can apply this idea to something you are

① bombard [bɔm'b:d] v. 轰炸；不断攻击；向……连续提问题
② insurmountable [,ins'mauntbl] adj. 不能克服的；无法逾越的

美丽语录

The God only arranges a happy ending. If it is not happy, it means that it is not the final result.

上天只会安排快乐的结局。如果不快乐，说明还不是最后结局。

我喜欢的一张海报上说："生活是个测试。仅仅是个测试。如果你能直面人生，你便早会被告知何去何从。"每当我想起这颇有点幽默的人生哲理，它便提醒我不要把生活看得那么严肃。

当你把生活和它的许多挑战看成一个测试，或一系列测试，你便会将你面对的每一问题看作一次成长的机会，看作一次更深刻地发现生活的机会。不管你是否深陷种种问题、责任，甚至是不可逾越的障碍的围攻，当你将这一切看作测试，你总有机会获胜——就是说你能超越挑战。但另一方面，如果你视你面临的每一个新问题为一场严肃的、为了生存必须赢得的战斗，那你恐怕就踏上了一个十分艰辛的旅程。你唯一的快乐时光便是一切都尽如人意。但我们都知道，一切尽如人意的概率是多么低。

作为试验，看看你能否把这一观念应用到你必须处理的某件事情中。

forced to deal whit. Perhaps you have much pressure from your parents or you have a demanding boss. See if you can **redefine**[①] the issue, you face from being a "problem" to being a test. Rather than struggling with your issue see if there is something you can learn from it. Ask yourself, "Why is this an issue, in my life? What would it mean and what would be involved to rise above it? Could I possibly look at this issue any differently? Can I see it as a test of some kind?

If you give this strategy a try you may be surprised at your changed responses. It will become far more acceptable to you to accept thing as they are.

① redefine ['ri:di'fain] v. 对……再加以解说；再给……下定义

也许你感觉有来自父母的很大压力，或者你有一位十分严苛的老板。看看你能否将你面临的“问题”重新定义为“测试”。与其和你的问题搏斗，不如看看你能从中学到点什么。问问自己：“为什么这成了我生活中的一个问题？它意味着什么，超越它我需要做些什么？我能否换个角度看看这问题？我能否视之为某种测试？”

如果你尝试用一下这个策略，你会惊奇地发现你对它的反应全变了。它将使你学会按照事情的本来面目接受它们。

Minnesota Dreamer

明尼苏达州的梦想家

◎ San Martin

Even if I did not have a dream, I always had a plan. In college, I learned to be responsible and organized and to set goals that I could attain. Then everything changed. I will never forget my final week from college last year. Days away from graduation and miles away from home, I was diagnosed with a brain tumor. I left the hospital alone, in **devastation**①. Unsure of what my future would hold, I shed countless tears. Life suddenly became an unforeseeable thing, and I could not know what to do. Although close friends eased the pain, I could not hide from them my fear of facing death. Somehow, I managed to complete the exams in spite of my jangled nerves.

I began to feel different from everyone else, since my friends were graduating, celebrating, and eager to move on to new chapters in their lives. But I could not join them and celebrate with them. I especially found it interesting to see how others around me dealt with my news. Some acted suddenly distant for lack of words, some dramatized the whole thing, and some acted perfectly normal, which felt the most comfortable for me.

① devastation [ˌdevəs'teiʃən] n. 蹂躏；荒废

美丽语录

You are braver than you believe, stronger than you seem, and smarter than you think.

你比你想象中更勇敢，比你看起来更强大，也比你以为的更聪明。

我一直都有计划，即使是在我一个梦想都没有的时候。在大学期间，我学会了做人要有责任感，做事要有条理性，要树立切实可行的目标。从那以后，一切都发生了变化。去年，大学毕业前的一周是我终生难忘的日子。毕业前几天，我在离家很远的地方被诊断出患有脑瘤。我陷入了绝望，独自从医院里跑了出来。我不知道未来会是什么样子，泪水止不住地掉下来。生活突然间变得无法预测，我感到茫然。虽然好友的安慰减轻了我的痛苦，然而，我无法在他们面前掩饰对死亡的恐惧。尽管烦乱至极，不知道为什么，我还是完成了考试。

我的朋友们都在忙着毕业、庆祝，急切地迈向新的生活，我却无法加入他们，不能和他们一起庆祝，我逐渐发现自己变得与众不同了。我饶有兴趣地观察身边的人对我生病消息的反应。一些人因为不知道跟我说些什么而远离我；一些人的反应极具戏剧性；还有一些人好像什么都没有发生过，当我面对这些人时，却感到十分自在。

Within days, I had packed up all of my college belongings and headed home with my family ready to face this unexpected hurdle. I immediately turned to my best friend from high school. She had gone through cancer in our senior year, and because of watching her courageously overcome so many obstacles four years before, I knew she could give me the **fuel**① I needed for my own battle.

As my surgery date to remove the tumor got closer, I was experiencing intense physical pain. Part of me wanted it over with and the other part of me was coming **unglued**②. The wall of strength I had built was crumbling. I was so angry that I had to go through this when all those around me were going on with their lives. I spent a lot of time asking, why me?

But something wonderful started happening in the midst of all this. I began to see all the beauty around me in a wholly new way. The smallest things that I neglected before started to catch my eyes. I noticed how colorful and serene a sunset could be when you took time to enjoy it. Blades of grass cascading along hillsides looked a brighter shade of green. A small child's laughter became an instant remedy for a bad day.

Miraculously, I woke up from surgery grateful to be alive and well. Words cannot describe the happiness I felt at that special moment—to be given a second chance. My recovery was a long process as I learned to walk again and so simple tasks. I remember when I went home and studied my bald head for the first time. It shouldn't have surprised me, but it did! Ironically, a month before I knew I had a tumor, I cut my long hair short and donated it to the American Cancer Society. I discovered there is a huge difference between short and bald!

① fuel ['fjuəl] n. 动力；刺激；燃料

② unglued [ʌn'glu:d] adj. 身心失调的；心烦意乱的

几天后，我收拾好学校里的所有行李，回家与家人一起面对这意想不到的不幸。到家后，我马上去找高中时代最好的朋友。她在高三那年患了癌症，四年前，我曾亲眼目睹她勇敢地克服了所有磨难，我知道，她能够给我与疾病作战的勇气。

离肿瘤切除手术的日子越来越近时，剧烈的病痛折磨着我的身体。我一边想随它去，一边又感到极度烦乱。我所建立起来的精神支柱濒临崩溃的边缘。身边的其他人都健康地活着，而我却要遭受病痛的折磨，我变得非常愤怒。很多时候我都在问自己：为什么会是我？

就在这时，一些令人惊奇的事情发生了。这使我开始以全新的眼光看待周围所有美好的事物。我开始关注那些极其微小的事情，曾经，我忽略了它们的存在。我注意到，花一点时间去享受落日，你就会发现那是多么的缤纷和平静；从山腰飘落下来的绿色草片，看起来是那么鲜亮；只要听听小孩子的笑声，一整天糟糕的煎熬马上就会消失得无影无踪。

我从手术中醒来后，感激自己健康地活了下来，这真是不可思议。我获得了第二次生命，那一刻我的心中充满了无以言表的幸福感。我要重新学习走路，做一些简单的任务，我的身体完全恢复是一个漫长的过程。记得，在回到家里后，我第一次仔细地看自己光秃秃的脑袋，这令我惊讶，其实，我本不该如此。具有讽刺意味的是，在我被诊断为患有脑瘤的一个月之前，我刚把头发剪短捐给了美国癌症学会。我发现，短发和光头简直有着天壤之别！

Life can sure throw a good curve ball when you least expect it. Yet I have had this new start, and I am enjoying every minute of it. I used to hear people say you should dream the unimaginable, and I always preferred to plan instead. Now, dreaming big and following my heart's desire without knowing how it will end up is the only thing I have time to do.

生活会在你意想不到的时候捉弄你，这是必然的。既然我有了这个新的开始，我就要享受生命的每一分钟。过去我常听人们说，你要去梦想那些不可能的事情，而我却总是宁愿按部就班。现在，心怀梦想，跟着内心的渴望向前走，而不必考虑结果如何，成了余下的时间里我要做的唯一一件事。

We Are on a Journey
人在旅途

◎ Henry Van Dyke

Wherever you are, and whoever you may be, there is one thing in which you and I are just alike, at this moment, and in all the moments of our existence. We are not at rest; we are on a journey. Our life is not a mere fact; it is a movement, a tendency, a **steady**①, ceaseless progress towards an unseen goal.

We are gaining something, or losing something, every day. Even when our position and our character seem to remain **precisely**② the same, they are changing. For the mere advance of time is a change. It is not the same thing to have a bare field in January and in July. The season makes the difference. The limitations that are childlike in the child are childish in the man. Everything that we do is a step in one direction or another. Even the failure to do something is in itself a deed. It sets us forward or backward. The action of the negative pole of a **magnetic**③ needle is just as real as the action of the positive pole. To decline is to accept—the other alternative.

Are you nearer to your port today than you were yesterday? Yes, —you must be a little nearer to some port or other; for since your ship was first launched upon the sea of life you have never been still for a single moment; the sea is too deep, you could not find an anchorage if you would; there can be no pause until you come into port.

---

① steady ['stedi] adj. 稳固的；不变的

② precisely [pri'saisli] adv. 恰恰，正好

③ magnetic [mæg'netik] adj. 磁铁的；有磁性的

美丽语录

We'd better struggle for the future rather than regret for the past.

与其后悔过去，不如奋斗将来。

无论你身在何处，无论你是谁，此时此刻，有一件事对你我而言都是相同的，而且只要我们活着，这个共同点就存在。那就是，我们并非停留不前，而是人在旅途。我们的生命不仅仅是一个纯粹的事件，而是一种运动，一种趋势，是向一个看不见的目标不断奋进。

每天，我们都有所得，也有所失。即便我们的位置和角色看似与原来无异，但实际上也在时时变化。因为时间的推移本身就是一种变化。对于同一片荒地来说，在一月和七月是截然不同的，季节造成了这种差异。能力的局限在孩子身上被视为天真烂漫，而在大人身上则是幼稚的表现。我们所做的一切都是朝着某个方向迈进了一步。即使是失败本身，也是有所得的。失败可以催人奋进，也可以让人一蹶不振。磁针负极的作用与正极的作用都是一样真实的。拒绝也是一种接受——不过是另一种选择罢了。

你今天比昨天更接近你的港口了吗？是的，你肯定离某个港口更近了；因为自从你的航船从生命之海上启航的那一刻起，你没有哪一刻是静止的。大海如此深邃，即便你想停泊，也找不到地方；只有当你驶入自己的港口，你才能停止下来。

Which Group Do You Belong to
80、90后的你属于哪一族

啃老族 the NEET group

"啃老族"又称尼特族，NEET的全称是（Not currently engaged in Employment, Education or Training），最早使用于英国，之后渐渐也在其他国家出现；它是指不升学、不就业，终日无所事事、有劳动力但仍依靠父母供养的一群年轻人。

闪居族 flash cohabitants

"闪居"即"闪电同居"的意思。在英语中，已经有一个词cohabit表示"同居"的意思，那么"同居族"即为cohabiters，而"闪居族"就可译为lightening cohabiters。

穷忙族 the working poor

"穷忙族"来自英文单词working poor，原意是指那些薪水不多，整日奔波劳动，却始终无法摆脱"贫困"状态的人。但是随着"穷忙族"队伍逐渐壮大，这个定义又发展成一种即使每天努力工作，但在日益增长的消费状况下依旧没有积蓄、无力置产，既忙又穷的工作穷人。

走班族 walking commuters

"走班族"是指为了锻炼身体而放弃交通工具，自愿步行上下班的人。在英语中，commuters本来是指那些乘车上下班的人，但"走班"一词却无直接的相应词汇。按照"走班族"所含的含义，该词译为walking commuters。

慢活族 slow walkers

"慢活族"是指追求慢节奏生活的人，其准确译文应该是persons with slow-pace life，但这种译法却使译文失去了词汇术语的特点。所以我们以象征的手法将该词译为slow walker（行走步伐缓慢的人）。

飞鱼族 the flying fish

"飞鱼族"指的是在国内已取得不俗成绩，但毅然放下一切，到国外名校求学的特殊中国群体。因其特定意义在英语中并未有现成的对应词汇，故将其直译为 the flying fish。"飞鱼族"源自禹风的一部小说《巴黎飞鱼》，既比喻跃出自己所熟悉的本国行业，试图在欧美天空飞翔的这一冒险举动，又比喻"本身是鱼，却一心想飞"的心态。

酷抠族 cool carls

"酷抠族"指的是高学历、高收入却追求简朴生活方式的社会族群。该词的涵义并非是说他们对于金钱和待人处事真正意义上的"抠门"，所以不宜将其直译为 cool miser，而译为 cool carl。这样，既有"酷"（cool）的超逸，也有凡人（carl）的简约，而且读音也与"酷抠"相近。

月光族 moonlight clan

"月光族"指将每月赚的钱都花光的人，一般都是年轻一代，随意性的开支是月光族产生的根源。与此同时，该词也用来形容赚钱不多，每月收入仅可以维持每月基本开销的一类人。这个词是一个中性词，没有绝对的褒贬意之分。

闪婚族 flash marriage group

"闪婚"是指两人在短暂的相识后，未经过长时间的交往和相互了解而确立婚姻关系的一种快速婚姻形式。对于"闪婚族"而言，即用最快的速度来完成从恋爱、产生爱情到结婚的漫长过程，媒体描述他们为"几秒钟可以爱上一个人，几分钟就能谈完一场恋爱，数小时内可以决定终身大事，一周便能踏上红地毯。"

波波族 BoBos

波波，译自 BoBo，指的是那些高学历、收入丰厚、追求生活享受、崇尚自由解放、积极进取的具有较强独立意识的一类人。BoBos 一词源于一本名为《BoBos in Paradise》(《天堂中的布波族》) 的书，由 Bourgeois 和 Bohemian 两词合并而成。BoBo 人视自己为一种格调生活的象征。

一起走过的日子

Friend is someone who can see the truth and pain in you even when you are fooling everyone else.

真正的朋友就是，当你蒙蔽了所有人的眼睛，也能看穿你真实的样子和心底的痛楚。

Compassion Is in the Eyes
眼里的同情

◎ Ki. Athelene

It was bitter cold evening in northern Virginia many years ago. The old man's beard was glazed by winter's frost while he waited for a ride across the river. The wait seemed endless. His body became numb and stiff from the **frigid**① north wind.

He heard the faint, steady rhythm of approaching hooves galloping along the frozen path. Anxiously, he watched as several horsemen rounded the bend. He let the first one passed by without any effort to get his attention, then another passed by, and another. Finally, the last rider neared the spot where the old man sat like a snow **statue**②. As this one draw near, the old man caught the rider's eye and said, "Sir, would you mind giving an old man a ride to the other side? There doesn't appear to be a passage way by foot."

Reining his horse, the rider replied, "Sure thing. Hop aboard." Seeing the old man was unable to lift his half-frozen body from the ground, the horseman dismounted and helped the old man onto the horse. The horseman took the old

① frigid ['fridʒid] adj. 寒冷的，严寒的

② statue ['stætju:] n. 雕像，塑像

美丽语录

I'll take an earnest person over a hip person every day, because hip is short term. Earnest is long term.

我会帮助一个真诚的人，而不会帮助一个时髦的人。因为时髦是短暂的，惟真诚永恒。

很多年以前，在弗吉尼亚北部的一个严寒的夜晚，一位老人站在河边等待有人可以带他过河，他的胡子都被冬霜染白了。等待似乎没有尽头。他的身体在寒冷的北风中冻得僵直麻木。

他听到冰冻的路面上传来渐渐接近的马蹄声，遥远而又平稳。他焦急地张望着几个骑马的人转过路弯。第一个人过来，他丝毫没有叫他，接着又来一个，再一个。最后，最后一个骑马的人过来，老人已经像一个雪人了。这个人越走越近，老人的目光与他相接了，老人说："先生，你介意搭我这个老头过河吗？似乎这里没有能走过去的地方。"

骑手停下了马儿，回答道："当然。上马吧。"看到老人无法挪动他已被冻僵的身体，骑手跳下来，把老人扶上马。他不仅把老人送过了河，还

man not just across the river, but to his destination, which was just a few miles away.

As they neared the tiny but cozy cottage, the horseman's curiosity caused him to inquire, "Sir, I notice you let several other riders pass by without making an effort to secure a ride. Then I came up and you immediately asked me for a ride. I am curious why, on such a bitter night, you would wait and ask the last rider. What if I had refused and left you here?"

The old man lowered himself slowly down from the horse, looked the rider straight in the eyes, and replied, "I have been around these here parts for some time. I **reckon**[①] I know people pretty good." The old-timer continued, "I looked into the eyes of the other riders and immediately saw there was no concern for my situation. It would have been useless even to ask them for a ride. But when I looked into your eyes, that your gentle spirit would welcome the opportunity to give me assistance in my time of need."

Those heart-warming comments touched the horseman deeply. "I'm so grateful for what you have said," he told the old man. "May I never get too busy in my own affairs that I fail to respond to the needs of others with kindness and compassion."

With that, Thomas Jefferson turned his horse around and made his way back to the White House.

① reckon ['rekən] v. 认为，把……看作

把老人带到了仅仅几英里远的目的地。

当他们快要到达老人很小却温馨的房舍时，骑马人终于好奇地问道：“先生，我注意到你让好几个骑马的人过去了，却不叫他们搭你一程。然后我过来了，你马上就问我可否。我很奇怪，在这样一个寒冷的夜晚，你为什么要等到最后一个人才问呢？如果我拒绝了你，留你一个人在这里怎么办？”

老人慢慢下马，直望着骑马人的眼睛，说道：“我已经在那儿等了一阵子。我相信自己看人很准。”老人继续说，“我看那些人的眼睛，他们没有流露出关心我的处境。这样即便问他们也是徒劳的。但当我看你的眼睛时，有很明显的善意和同情。我知道你本性善良，会因为我的需要而给我帮助。”

这些热情洋溢的话深深打动了骑马人。“我很感激你说的一切，”他对老人说，“我希望今后，不能因为繁忙的工作而无视对他人的怜悯和善心。”

说完后，托马斯·杰弗逊调转马头，向白宫方向骑去。

People Come into Your Life
你生活中的人们

◎ Alvin C. Romer

People come into your life for a reason, a season, or a lifetime. When you **figure out**[①] which it is, you know exactly what to do.

When someone is in your life for a reason, it is usually to meet a need you have expressed outwardly or inwardly. They have come to assist you through a difficulty, to provide you with guidance and support, to aid you physically, emotionally, or spiritually. They may seem like a godsend, and they are. They are there for the reason you need them to be. Then, without any wrong-doing on your part or at an inconvenient time, this person will say or do something to bring the relationship to an end.

Sometimes they die.

Sometimes they walk away.

Sometimes they act up or out and force you to take a stand.

What we must realize is that our need has been met, our desire fulfilled; their work is done. The prayer you sent up has been answered and it is now time to move on.

① figure out 算出，想出，理解

美丽语录

It is not easy to meet each other in such a big world.

世界这么大，能遇见，不容易。

人们走进你的生活，或者是为了一个原因，或者他们只停留一段时期，或者他们永远与你相随。一旦明晓其中究竟，你就知道该如何面对他们了。

当有的人因为某个原因出现在你的生活中，通常他们填补了你内在或外在流露出来的需要：帮你渡过难关，指点和支持你，切实地在身体上、情感上、精神上帮助你。他们有若上天所赐，确实如此。他们出现是因为你需要他们。然后，在一个你尢可引咎或不便的时候，这人说了什么或者做了什么令你们终止了友谊。

有时候他们离开人世。

有时候他们离你而去。

有时候他们冒出歪理而逼得你要奋起反抗。

我们必需认识到，自己的需要已经满足了，愿望已经实现了，他们的工作也就完成了。你的祈祷得到了回应，接着的是要继续前行。

When people come into your life for a season, it is because your turn has come to share, grow, or learn. They may bring you an experience of peace or make you laugh. They may teach you something you have never done. They usually give you an unbelievable amount of joy. Believe it! It is real! But, only for a season.

Lifetime relationships teach you lifetime lessons; those things you must build upon in order to have a solid emotional foundation. Your job is to accept the lesson, love the person (any way); and put what you have learned to use in all other relationships and areas of your life. It is said that love is blind but friendship is **clairvoyant**①.

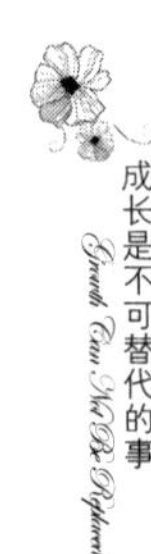

① clairvoyant [klɛr'vɔler'ənt] n. 有超人之目力或洞察力的

有的人在你的生活中只会停留一段时期，那是因为你到了这样的一个时候：成长、学习，并和别人一起分享你的世界。他们让你体会平和，也让你欢笑。他们可能也教会你做一些从没做过的事情。他们常能给你带来无数欢乐。相信这一点！这是真的！可这，只能维持一段时间。

持续一生的情谊将令你终生受益；一点一滴地努力吧，建造一个坚不可摧的感情基础。你要做的只是去接受经验，无论如何对一生相随的人付出关爱，并将你所学到应用到生命中的其他关系和方方面面中。爱情令人盲目，而友谊能让人醒醐灌顶，据说如此。

The Grass Is Always Green Right Under Your Feet
脚下的草地才是最绿的

◎ Sherri

Have you ever thought life would be better anywhere other than where you are right now? Maybe some of your thoughts go something like this:

Life will be better once I'm out of debt.

I can't wait until I'm retired because then I can do what I want when I want.

If only I lived somewhere warm I could exercise all year round and I would be so fit.

If I could just lose 10 pounds I know I would feel better.

Truth is some of your problems may go away once you have met all of your "if only's" and "better when's" but it won't make the perfect life that fairy tales are made of. New problems will arise and you'll likely find yourself wishing for this "perfect" life to be different still. We can only imagine that the grass will be greener on the other side because it's only when we live it do we actually see it for what it really is.

Whatever ideal you have in mind about an alternate lifestyle, location, financial situation etc ... rest assured that each one will be met with its own unique set of problems.

美丽语录

Don't forget what to do and where to go you have promised yourself no matter how difficult and hard it will be.

别忘了答应自己要做的事情，别忘了答应自己要去的地方，无论有多难，有多远。

你曾否有过这样的想法——无论如何，别处的生活都比此处的更好？或许你是这样想的：

一旦还清债务，生活就会更好。

我急不可耐地想要退休，那时就可以随时做我想做的事了。

如果能生活在一个温暖的地方，我就可以一年四季坚持锻炼，我会更健康。

如果我可以减掉 10 磅的体重，我会感觉更好。

问题在于许多问题会在你实现所有“如果”和“会更好”之后得到解决，但那绝对不是童话故事中制造的完美生活。新的问题又会出现，你仍会发现自己希望对“完美”生活加以改变。我们只能想象别处的草地比此处的更绿，因为，只有当我们生活在此处时，我们才能看到它的真面目。

只有当心目中不同的生活方式、居住地、财务状况等都体验过后，才会确信每种生活都会遇到专属于它的独特问题。

So what can you do about this? Choose to be content **with**[1] what you already have.

Look around you and be truly grateful for all that you see. Realize that there are people less fortunate than you and right now, rightly or wrongly, they are wishing for your exact lifestyle. Think back to 2 years ago, what were you wishing for then? Where did you want to be? Odds are you were largely wishing to be right where you are now. Life happens so gradually that you tend to lose all perspective of achievements, growth and progress.

It's great to dream big. But those dreams should not cloud the greatness you have in front of you right now. Consider the truth in the grass being the greenest right under your feet.

① be content with 满足于

那你该怎么应对呢？试着满意你已有的生活。

环视周围，真诚地感激你看到的一切。认识到周围还有比你不幸的人，他们正在或对或错地追逐你当下的生活方式。回想两年前，那时你的愿望是什么？你想去哪儿？很可能那时你期盼的就是现在的自己。生活常常会使你逐渐遗失所有对目标的憧憬、成长和进步。

敢于梦想固然好。但这些梦想不应该遮蔽自己现在的成就。要知道，现在你脚下的草才是最绿的。

The Old Man and the Rose
老人与玫瑰

◎ Heino Molls

During the mid 1950s when I was a kid, my dad worked in a furniture shop at Spadina and Queen in downtown Toronto. Sometimes, I got to go to the shop with him and I made a bit of pocket change running to the restaurant and getting coffee for everybody. I would pass the rest of the day away just hanging around the store, not doing much of anything and not paying much attention to all the hustle and bustle of people and things that were all around me.

One day, as my dad and I were driving to the shop, I looked out the passenger window of the car and I saw an old man standing at the street corner. For some reason, our eyes met and held for about twenty seconds as we went by the corner. There was nothing fearful about this man but it was a significant encounter for me. Up to that point in my life, I had given no thought to anyone I saw on the street, in stores or anywhere else. My life was my family and my friends on the block and that was it. I had no interest in anyone beyond that circle.

But I was intrigued by that old man. For the first time I had an **empathy**[①] and an interest in what that person was all about. What kind of life had he lived?

---

① empathy ['empəθi] n. 神入；移情作用；同理心

美丽语录

For every minute you are angry with someone, you lose 60 seconds of happiness that you can never get back.

对别人生气 1 分钟，就失去了自己人生中 60 秒无可挽回的快乐。

20 世纪 50 年代中期的时候，我还只是个孩子，爸爸在多伦多市区司帕蒂娜街与皇后街交汇处的一家家具店工作。有时我会跟他上店里去，还帮大家跑餐馆、买咖啡，从而挣点零用钱。余下的时间我会在家具店的附近转悠，无所事事，也不太在意周围纷繁嘈杂的各种人和事。

一天，爸爸和我开车到店里去的时候，我透过乘客座旁的车窗，看见那个街角处站着一位老人。出于某种原因，当车子拐过街角时，我们四目相对了，并且持续了大约 20 秒钟。这个老人没有什么令人害怕的地方，但这次相遇对我而言意义重大。在人生的那个结点之前，我从未留意过任何一个我在街上、在商店里或在其他地方看见的人。我的生活就只有我的家人和同个街区的朋友，仅此而已。我对那个生活圈以外的任何人都不感兴趣。

然而，我却对那个老人感兴趣。我第一次用了心思，对那个人的一切感到好奇。他的生活曾经是怎样的呢？他这辈子去过哪些地方呢？就在我

Where had he been in his time? How had he come to this corner just at the moment I was going by?

Over the years I had long forgotten about this old man, but he came to mind for me recently and I remembered those twenty seconds or so that I looked into the eyes of a stranger and wondered what he was all about.

It seems we are all so busy these days. There are so many details, so many calls to make and so many things to look after that we barely have time for sincere and genuine interest in others.

We are inundated by warnings from great thinkers in our society encouraging us to "stop and smell the roses". But I'm afraid it has taken me decades to really appreciate the wisdom of these words.

If I ever have the opportunity to speak to a young person today, I do my best to convey this message. But unfortunately, young people are too busy to heed good advice. Much like I was so many years ago. Youth indeed is so often wasted on the young.

If I had the chance, I would tell young people to stop what they are doing and look around. I would tell them to try as hard as they could to fully understand what is right in their line of sight, what is in the range of their hearing at the moment, what is in their immediate reach and grasp.

I would like so much to tell people, especially young people, that if you are thoughtless and indifferent to others on your road in life, then you are missing life itself. Do not be intrusive or tactless, for heaven's sake, but take a moment and ask someone, how did you come here or how did you get into this business?

No matter what that person tells you, their answer will make you richer. You can grow emotionally, you can excel as a person and you can be wealthy by

要经过的那一刻，他是怎样来到这个街角的呢?

许多年来，我早就忘记了这位老人，可最近他又出现在我的脑海里，我记起了那 20 秒钟四目相对的瞬间，当时我看着一个陌生人的眼睛，想要知道关于他的一切。

如今，我们似乎都太忙了。我们总有那么多的琐事要操心，那么多的电话要打，那么多的事情要料理，几乎没有时间再对别人产生真挚的关心。

我们经常得到社会上那些伟大思想家的告诫，他们敦促我们“停下手中的活，去闻闻玫瑰花的香味”。但是，我恐怕花了几十年的时间才真正读懂这句话所蕴含的智慧。

如今，如果我有机会和年轻人交谈，我就会尽力传达这个意思。可遗憾的是，年轻人都太忙了，无暇留意金玉良言，这很像多年前的我。诚然，青春往往就是在年轻的时候被白白浪费掉了.

如果有机会，我会告诉年轻人放下手中的活，看看四周。我会告诉他们尽可能努力地去弄明白，他们视线所及看到的究竟是什么，那一刻在他们听觉范围内传入耳朵的是什么，他们眼下够得着又抓得住的是什么。

我很乐意告诉人们，特别是年轻人，如果你在人生路上对他人漠不关心、冷漠相待，那么，与你擦肩而过的就是生活本身。看在老天的份上，不要干涉别人的私事或者说不得体的话，但你可以花上一些时间问问某个人，他是怎么来到这里的或者他是怎么踏入这一行。

无论那个人告诉你什么，他们的回答都将使你更加富有。只要你能重

every measure if you just appreciate the gifts that people and life all around you are ready to give right at this moment just by their simple presence.

We should appreciate that great **symphonies**① were written from only seven simple notes that God gave the entire universe. We should know that great works of art are measured by the emotions they evoke, not just how they look next to the plant stand.

We should never forget that heartache cannot be cured but can be eased by someone willing to give genuine sympathy. The true greatness of joy can only be known when it is shared with others.

Recently, I attended a trade show at the convention centre in downtown Toronto. During the lunch break I went to a book sale along the trendy Queen West area. I was thinking about returning to the show or carrying on my walk when I realized I was standing at the corner of Spadina and Queen. At that moment a car went by and I caught the eye of a young boy looking at me from the passenger window. We looked at each other for about twenty seconds before the car disappeared around the corner. I wondered if that boy was thinking about what sort of person I was.

And I realized that I was now an old man. Like the man I saw so many years ago.

I wondered if 50 years had just simply flashed by or whether that boy and I had just simply changed places in the span of 20 seconds.

Before I returned to the trade show, I stopped at a florist. I bought a rose and put it in the lapel of my jacket. For some reason, I felt it was the most important thing I would do for the rest of the day.

① symphony ['simfəni] n. 交响乐；交响乐团

视你周围的人和生活赐予的权力，你就能在情感上变得成熟，你就能成为一个优秀的人，你就能在每个方面都很富有。

我们应该明白：伟大的交响乐是用上帝赐予全世界的 7 个简单音符谱写而成的。我们应该懂得：伟大的艺术品是由它们自身所唤起的情感来衡量的，而不只是由它们在园艺架旁的外观所决定的。

我们必须永远记得：心痛无药可治，却会因为某个人自愿给予真心的同情而减轻。与人分享的喜悦才是最伟大的喜悦。

最近，我参加了在多伦多市区会展中心举办的交易会。午餐休息的时候，我去了一个书市，就在时尚新潮的皇后西街那儿。我正在犹豫着是回到交易会还是继续向前走，这时我意识到自己就站在司帕蒂娜街与皇后街相交的街角上。正在这时，一辆小汽车从我面前驶过，我与一个从乘客座车窗朝外看的小男孩四目交汇。我们彼此打量了大约 20 秒钟，然后汽车转过街角消失了。我不知道那个男孩是否在想我是个什么样的人。

我意识到自己如今已是老人，就像多年以前我见到的那个人一样。

我迷惑了，难道 50 年就这样转瞬即逝了？还是我和那个男孩在 20 秒的时间里互换了位置？

在回交易会的路上，我走进一家花店，买了一朵玫瑰别在夹克的翻领上。出于某种原因，我觉得这是那天余下的时光里我要做的最重要的事。

A Grandfather's Touch

感受异国的阳光

◎ Tom Brown

What day is it today? Is it Tuesday or Thursday? This thought raced through her mind as she sat back with her students going over the lesson that never seemed to end. Didn't I just do this yesterday? Or was it a year ago? Hell, everything seemed to jumble together anymore. "Miss Smith, can I go to the bathroom?"Jorge asked, as he proceeded to jump from one foot to another, holding himself. How many times have I heard this? She wondered as she **abruptly**① said, "Yes" and watched as he raced out of the room.

Sitting at the table she gazed at her students while thinking of what she would do after work. Maybe I'll go to the gym or stop at the market for something to eat tonight. Mechanically she continued with her lesson on the short letter "a" with her students. "The letter 'a' makes what sound?" "A, a, a..." the students sang together going through the empty motions. The clock dragged away the minutes teasing her with the **tediousness**② of the day.

Won't it end? She thought as the phone rang out its morse code for her

① abruptly [ə'brʌptli] adv. 唐突地，突然地

② tediousness ['tidiəsnis] n. 乏味，无聊

美丽语录

If you would be loved, love and be lovable.

想要别人爱你的话，就要去爱别人，做一个可爱的人。

今天周几，周二还是周四？她一直带着学生们进行那似乎永无休止的复习。这件事我好像昨天刚刚做过？或者去年做过？烦死了，怎么都赶到一块儿了。“史密斯小姐，我可以去下洗手间吗？”正要迈腿跑出去的乔治，停下来问道。我是第几次听到这样的话了？她想着，随口答道，“好。”然后她看着他跑出了教室。

她坐在桌旁凝视着学生们，脑子却不停地在想下班后该做些什么。我今晚该去健身房或是经过市场时买点儿吃的。她机械地继续上她的课，给学生讲字母“a”。“‘a’怎么读？”“a，a，a……”学生们异口同声干巴巴地读着。时间一分一秒地过去，似乎在嘲笑她这乏味的一天。

该下课了吧？正想着，教室的电话响了。她叹了一口气，站起来，走

room. Sighing she stood up and walked through the maze of students desks to get to the phone. Picking up the receiver the other voice seemed a hundred miles away. Oh, how I wish I were anywhere but here. Her mind wandered to the hot exotic beach of Cabo, Mexico, where she had spent her last summer break. She still remembered the cool breezes that caressed her skin as she lay on the gritty sand.

"Miss Smith, did you hear me?" the secretary annoyingly asked her. "Oh, sorry. What did you say?" "Can you send Carla to the office?" the secretary impatiently asked. "Oh, course." she replied as she hung up the phone. She turned from the phone and yelled out Carla's name. Carla, who was one of the many who always seemed so needy that were in her class this year. Carla looked up from her desk, her hair hanging like a matted displaced doll. Her face was lined with dirt that gave her the appearance of one of those munchkins from the Wizard of Oz. "You need to go to the office." She said while Carla slowly rose from her desk. "Why do I have to go?" whined Carla. "It's between you and the office—just go up." She hastily turned her back as Carla walked out of the room. Like having free school uniforms is the answer. It would be nice if just once someone called saying something nice or thanking me for all the endless crap I have to deal with. With a sigh she walked back to her other students who were clustered at the back table patiently waiting her return.

The rest of the afternoon blurred into one long endless repetition. Finally the bell rang as a relief. As she led her students out the door they walked behind her as baby chicks returning to their fold. She noticed that their mother hens clucked to them behind the iron gate. As she proceeded to walk down the corridor, the air, which rose with the musical tingle of Spanish coloring everything that touched it,

过学生迷宫一样的课桌去接电话。话筒那端的声音似乎传自百里之外。哦，我多希望我现在不在这里啊。她的思绪飞到了异国情调浓郁的墨西哥卡波海滩，去年她在那儿度过了愉快的暑假。她慵懒地躺在沙滩上，阵阵微风轻吻她的肌肤，那种惬意的感觉，至今记忆犹新。

“史密斯小姐，你在听我讲话吗？”秘书不耐烦地问道。“哦，抱歉。刚才你说什么了？”“麻烦你让卡拉来我办公室一趟。”秘书更加不耐烦地说。“哦，当然可以。”说着，她挂断了电话。她转过身来叫卡拉的名字。卡拉是这个班上本年众多的贫困生之一。卡拉抬起头，松散的头发像一蓬乱草，满脸污垢，活像《绿野仙踪》里的一个稻草人。“你到办公室去一趟。”她对慢慢抬起头的卡拉说道。“为什么让我去？”卡拉嘀咕道。“让你去你就去——快去吧！”卡拉出去了，她匆忙地转回身。卡拉看样子是去领免费校服的。如果有人打电话来说些好话，或是对我做的这些令人讨厌的工作表示感谢，那该多好。她叹了口气，走回去，学生们都聚在后面的桌边耐心地等着她。

这极其单调的工作重复了一下午。最后，解放的铃声终于响了。她带着学生走出教室，就像母鸡带着鸡崽儿回窝似的。她看到学生的妈妈们都在铁门外热切地期待着。当她路过走廊时，满载西班牙音乐气息的空气迎面扑来。她欣慰地看着孩子们离开，也许是回到充满欢声笑语的家，而自己却不得不再次回到那无尽的单调乏味中。

greeted her. She watched with a touch of envy as the children left her to return to those homes that probably were filled with laughter and warmth while she would once again return to the same endless march of boredom.

"Senora, un momento por favor?" she turned her head and noticed the small shriveled man, his brown face lined with a map to places only he knew. "Thanks for helping my grandson Julio to read." the gentleman said in his faltering broken English. She immediately thought of Julio, who once as unreachable as a hardened walnut, slowly cracked opened to reveal the eager child inside. She thought of the inner struggle Julio must have had as he tried to make sense of the foreign letters and the sudden joy when he had unbroken the mysterious code. Was the grandfather the same? She looked up at this elderly gentleman, probably his grandfather, and quickly recognized the sameness of the two. "Gracias Senora" a weathered hand came out and firmly grasped hers with warmth that radiated from his soul to hers. Just as abruptly he removed his hand and left her. As he walked away she thought of that exotic sun and realized maybe it was closer to her than she thought.

“夫人，您好，可以打扰您几分钟吗？”她转过头来，一个窘迫的小个子男子出现在她面前，他那棕色的面庞布满皱纹。“谢谢您教我孙子胡里奥读书。”他用蹩脚的英语说道。她马上想起了胡里奥，外表看起来就像一个坚硬的核桃那么不易接近，后来渐渐地敞开了他充满渴盼的内心世界。她想胡里奥一定在暗下决心努力学好外语，并为自己能破解这神奇的密码而欢欣鼓舞。这位祖父也一样吗？她抬头看了看这位老人，也许是祖父，很快便找到了两人的共同之处。“谢谢您，夫人！”一只饱经沧桑的手，紧紧握住她的手，他的热情深深地感染了她。很快，他把手缩了回去，走开了。当他离开时，她想到了异国的阳光，而且也意识到，异国的阳光其实就近在咫尺。

Chain of Love
爱的锁链

◎ Steve Goodier

"How do you **account for**[①] your remarkable accomplishment in life?" Queen Victoria of England asked Helen Keller. "How do you explain the fact that even though you were both blind and deaf, you were able to accomplish so much?"

Ms. Keller's answer is a tribute to her dedicated teacher. "If it had not been for Anne Sullivan, the name of Helen Keller would have remained unknown."

According to speaker Zig Ziglar, "Little Annie" Sullivan, as she was called when she was young, was no stranger to hardship. She was almost sightless herself (due to a childhood fever) and was, at one time, diagnosed as hopelessly "insane" by her caregivers. She was locked in the basement of a mental institution outside of Boston. On occasion, Little Annie would violently attack anyone who came near. Most of the time she generally ignored everyone in her presence.

An elderly nurse believed there was hope, however, and she made it her mission to show love to the child. Every day she visited Little Annie. For the most part, the child did not **acknowledge**[②] the nurse's presence, but she still

① account for 说明……原因；证明
② acknowledge [ək'nɔlidʒ] v. 承认，致谢

美丽语录

Living is hope and you have it. In fact, there's no desperate plight but the person who is despairing to the situation.

活着就是希望，活着就有希望。世上没有绝望的处境，只有对处境绝望的人。

“你一生中获得如此卓越成就的原因是什么？”英国维多利女王曾问海伦·凯勒，“你又聋又盲，你是如何取得如此巨大的成就的？”

凯勒女士将这一切归功于她那富于奉献精神的老师。“如果没有安妮·沙利文，海伦·凯勒的名字也许永远不会为人所知。”

据金克·金克拉说，小安妮——沙利文年幼时的名字——可是没少经历苦难。因为儿时发高烧，她几乎双目失明，且一度被看护者们诊断为精神失常，无法医治。她被锁在波士顿城外一个精神医院的地下室里。有时，小安妮会狂暴攻击每一个靠近她的人，但多数时候，她则对身边的每一个人不理不睬。

尽管如此，一位上了年纪的护士认为仍有希望。她把爱护这个孩子作为自己的职责，每天都去看小安妮。大多数时候，这孩子都意识不到护士

continued to visit. The kindly woman left cookies for her and spoke words of love and encouragement. She believed Little Annie could recover, if only she were shown love.

Eventually, doctors noticed a change in the girl. Where they once witnessed anger and hostility, they now noted an emerging gentleness and love. They moved her upstairs where she continued to improve. Then the day finally came when this seemingly "hopeless" child was released.

Anne Sullivan grew into a young woman with a desire to help others as she, herself, was helped by the kindly nurse. It was she who saw the great potential in Helen Keller. She loved her, disciplined her, played with her, pushed her and worked with her until the flickering candle that was her life became a beacon of light to the world. Anne Sullivan worked wonders in Helen's life; but it was a loving nurse who first believed in Little Annie and lovingly transformed an uncommunicative child into a compassionate teacher.

"If it had not been for Anne Sullivan, the name of Helen Keller would have remained unknown." But if it had not been for a kind and dedicated nurse, the name of Anne Sullivan would have remained unknown. And so it goes. Just how far back does the chain of redemption extend? And how far forward will it lead?

Those you have sought to reach, whether they be in your family or elsewhere, are part of a chain of love that can extend through the generations. Your influence on their lives, whether or not you see results, is **immeasurable**[①]. Your legacy of dedicated kindness and caring can transform lost and hopeless lives for years to come.

---

① immeasurable [i'meʒərəbl] a. 不可计量的

的存在，但她仍旧不断地去看她。这位善良的女士给孩子留下饼干，对她说鼓励和慈爱的话语。她坚信，只要有爱，小安妮就一定能恢复。

终于，医生发现了小姑娘身上的变化。曾经他们目睹的是愤怒和敌意，但现在看到了逐渐显现的温顺和爱意。他们把她搬到了楼上，在那里，她的情况继续好转。终于有一天，这个看来无药可救的孩子出院了。

安妮·沙利文长成了一个大姑娘，她热切地渴望去帮助别人，就像她自己被那位善良的护士帮助一样。正是她看到了海伦·凯特身上的巨大潜质。她爱护她，教育她，和她一起玩耍，给她鼓励，和她一起工作，直到她生命微弱的烛光变成了照亮世界的灯塔。安妮·沙利文创造了海伦生命的奇迹，但首先是一位好心的护士相信小安妮，并慈爱地将一个无法交流的孩子变成了一个富有爱心的老师。

“如果没有安妮·沙利文，海伦·凯勒的名字也许永远不为人知。”但是如果没有那个好心且富于奉献精神的护士，安妮·沙利文的名字也会永远不为人所知。如此这般，这条救助的链条会绵延到哪里？它又会向前延伸多远？

那些你所想到的人，不管他们在你家里或是其他地方，都是这条在几代人间延续的爱的锁链上的一环。你对他们生命的影响，不管你是否看到结果，都是无法估量的。你所奉献的爱心与关怀，将会在未来的岁月中转变那些处于失落和绝望之中的生命。

阅读小课堂

How to get along with people
如何与他人相处

◎ Mark Tyrrell

1. Keep skid chains on your tongue; always say less than you think. Cultivate a low, persuasive voice. How you say it counts more than what you say.

2. Make promises sparingly, and keep them faithfully, no matter what it costs.

3. Never let an opportunity pass to say a kind and encouraging word to or about somebody. Praise good work, regardless of who did it. If criticism is needed, criticize helpfully, never spitefully.

4. Be interested in others, their pursuits, their work, their homes and families. Make merry with those who rejoice; with those who weep, mourn. Let everyone you meet, however humble, feel that you regard him as a person of importance.

5. Be cheerful. Don't burden or depress those around you by dwelling on your minor aches and pains and small disappointments. Remember, everyone is carrying some kind of a load.

6. Keep an open mind. Discuss but don't argue. It is a mark of a superior

1. 惜言如金。说的永远比想的少。养成低声说话，说有力量的话的习惯。怎么说比说什么更重要。

2. 慎做许诺。无论代价如何，诚心诚意信守诺言。

3. 永远不要错失机会向某人说饱含善意和激励的话。赞美做得好的工作，不管那是谁做的。如果需要批评，就做有益的批评，绝不要怀有恶意。

4. 关心他人，关心他们的追求，他们的工作，他们的家和家人。和那些快乐的人、哭泣和哀伤的人一起营造快乐。让你遇见的每个人，无论他多么卑微，都能感受到你对他的重视。

5. 要令人感到愉快。不要老是述说你微不足道的周身疼痛和失望沮丧，给你周围的人增加压力和苦恼。记住，每个人都担负了某种负担。

6. 虚心接受他人意见。可以讨论，但不要争论。能友善地表示不同意见是有心胸开阔的标志。

mind to be able to disagree without being disagreeable.

7. Let your virtues speak for themselves. Refuse to talk of another's vices. Discourage gossip. It is a waste of valuable time and can be extremely destructive.

8. Be careful of other's feelings. Wit and humor at the other person's expense are rarely worth it and may hurt when least expected.

9. Pay no attention to ill-natured remarks about you. Remember, the person who carried the message may not be the most accurate reporter in the world. Simply live so that nobody will believe them. Disordered nerves and bad digestion are a common cause of backbiting.

10. Don't be too anxious about the credit due you. Do your best, and be patient. Forget about yourself, and let others "remember." Success is much sweeter that way.

7. 让优点自己表现出来。拒绝谈论他人的缺陷。劝阻流言蜚语。那是宝贵时间的浪费，破坏性可能极强。

8. 照顾他人的感受。以损害他人为代价的风趣和幽默很不值得，可能会在不经意间伤害他人。

9. 不要太在意那些对你的流言蜚语。记住，传播信息的人可能不是世界上最实事求是的记者。随它去吧，不会有人相信的。神经过敏和承受力差是产生流言蜚语的常见原因。

10. 不要急于求得信任。尽最大努力，耐心等待。忘记你自己，让别人“记住”。这样获得的成功才愉悦。

重新遇见自己

Whether you are young or young at heart, it is never too late to change—or incorporate some new and better practices into your daily life.

不管你是真的风华正茂，或是心态年轻，改变，或让自己的生活吸收一些新的更好的尝试，永远为时不晚。

Broken Wings, Flying Heart
翅膀断了，我心飞翔

◎ Catherine

He lost his arms in an accident that claimed his father's life—who was the main source of support for the family. Since then, he has had to depend on the arms of his younger brother. For the sake of taking care of him, his younger brother became his shadow, never leaving him alone for years. Except for writing with his toes, he was completely unable to do anything in his life.

One late night, he suffered from **diarrhea**[①] and had to wake up his younger brother. His younger brother accompanied him into the toilet and then went back the dorm to wait. But being so tired, his younger brother fell asleep; leaving him on the toilet for two hours till the teacher on duty discovered him. As the two brothers grew up together, they had their share of problems and they would often quarrel. Then one day, his younger brother wanted to live separate from him, living his own life, as many normal people do. So he was heart-broken and didn't know what to do.

A similar misfortune **befell**[②] a girl, too. One night her mother, who suffered

① diarrhea [ˌdaiə'riə] n. 腹泻

② befall [bi'fɔːl] v. 发生，降临（尤指不幸）

美丽语录

The minute you think of giving up, think of the reason why you held on so long.

在你想要放弃的那一刻，想想为什么当初坚持走到了这里。

在一场车祸中，他失去了双臂，也失去了父亲，而父亲原是这个家的顶梁柱。从此，他不得不开始依靠弟弟稚嫩的双臂。为了照顾他，弟弟成了他的影子，几年来寸步不离他身边。而他除了能用脚趾写字，其他的生活琐事完全不能自理。

某天深夜里，他腹泻得厉害，不得不叫醒他的弟弟。他的弟弟帮助他进了厕所后，回到宿舍去等他。但是，由于太累了，他的弟弟睡着了，把他一个人留在厕所呆了两个小时，直到值班老师发现他。这对兄弟从小一起长大，一起承担着所有的困难，也会经常吵架。后来有一天，他弟弟想离开他，像许多正常人一样过自己的生活。他的心都碎了，更不知道接下来该怎么办。

同样的不幸也降临到一个女孩身上。有一天夜里，她患有慢性精神病

from chronic mental illness disappeared. So her father went out looking for her mother, leaving her alone at home. She tried to prepare meals for her parents, only to **overturn**① the kerosene light on the stove, resulting in a fire which took her hands away.

Though her elder sister who was studying in another city, showed her willingness to take care of her, she was determined to be completely independent. At school, she always studied hard. Most of all she learned to be self-reliant. Once she wrote the following in her composition: "I am lucky. Though I lost my arms, I still have legs; I am lucky. Though my wings are broken, my heart can still fly."

One day, the boy and the girl were both invited to appear on a television interview program. The boy told the TV host about his uncertain future at being left on his own, whereas the girl was full of enthusiasm for her life. They both were asked to write something on a piece of paper with their toes. The boy wrote: My younger brother's arms are my arms; while the girl wrote: Broken wings, flying heart.

They had both endured the same ordeal, but their different attitudes determined the nature of their lives. It is true that life is unpredictable. Disasters can strike at any time. How you handle misfortune when confronted with it, is the true test of your character. If you choose only to complain and escape from the ordeal, it will always follow you wherever you go. But if you decide to be strong, the hardship will turn out to be a fortune on which new hopes will arise.

① overturn [ˌəuvəˈtəːn] v. 翻倒，打翻

的母亲失踪了，于是她的父亲出去找她母亲，把她独自留在家里。她试着为父母准备饭菜，却把煤油灯打翻在炉子上，引发火灾，而火灾夺去了她的双手。

虽然她在另一个城市读书的姐姐表示愿意照顾她，她还是决定要完全靠自己。在学校里，她一直很努力地学习。最重要的是，她学会了自力更生。她曾在一篇作文里写道："我是幸运的，虽然失去了双臂，但我还有双腿；我是幸运的，虽然翅膀断了，但心依旧在飞翔。"

有一天，男孩和女孩都应邀参加一次电视采访节目。男孩对电视节目主持人谈起留给他的未来不禁感慨前途渺茫；而女孩，却对她未来的生活充满了热情。他们都被要求用脚趾在纸上写下点什么。男孩写下的是：弟弟的双手就是我的双手；而女孩写下的：翅膀断了，但我心飞翔。

他们都经历了同样的苦难，但不同的态度决定了他们不同的生活状态。生活是不可预测的，这是事实。灾害随时都可能降临。如何应对苦难，则是对你品格的真正考验。如果你选择了抱怨和逃避磨难，那么不管你走到哪里，它都会永远跟随你。但是，如果你决定要坚强，那么苦难将会成为一种财富，为你带来新希望。

A New Attitude to Gratitude
对待感激的新态度

◎ Michelle Blake

One of the nice things about having grown children is that I no longer have to bug them about writing thank-you notes. When they were little, all three would dictate thank-yous that I would include with drawings they'd made of their presents. By the time Eleanor, Sarah and Drew were old enough to write their own thank-you notes, however, they would do so only with much **prodding**[①].

"Have you written to thank Grandy for the book yet?" I'd ask. "What did you say to Aunt Dorothy about that top?" Invariably, I'd be met with mumbles and shrugs.

One year, in the days following Christmas, I'd grown weary of nagging. The children had become mother-deaf. Frustrated, I declared that no one would be allowed to play with a new toy or wear a new outfit until the appropriate thank-you notes had been mailed. Still they procrastinated and grumbled.

Something snapped. "Everyone into the car." I said.

"Where are we going?" Sarah asked, bewildered.

"To buy a Christmas present." But it's after Christmas, she protested.

① prodding [ˈprɔdiŋ] n. 刺激，敦促，推动

美丽语录

Sometimes you will never know the true value of a moment until it becomes a memory.

有时候，直到一些珍贵的时刻成为了回忆，你才会真正意识到它的价值所在。

孩子们长大了有这样一个好处：再也不用我去督促他们写感谢信了。我的三个孩子还小的时候，总是口述他们的感谢信，由我写下他们的话，并与他们作为礼物而画的画一起寄走。等埃莉诺、萨拉和德鲁长到能够自己写感谢信时，他们却又不愿意写，总是要我百般催促。

“你们写信感谢格兰迪送你们书了吗？”我问道，“还有多萝西姨妈送给你们陀螺，你们写了吗？”每一次，他们都是嘟哝着，摊手耸肩。

有一年，圣诞节刚过去几天，我不想再唠叨了。孩子们对妈妈的话也已变得充耳不闻。我非常沮丧，只得宣布，任何人都不准玩新玩具或穿新衣服，除非他们把该写的感谢信写好寄走。可他们依旧拖延着，抱怨不休。

我灵机一动，说，“你们都给我上车！”

“去哪儿？”萨拉困惑地问。

“买圣诞礼物。”可圣诞节已经过去了，她反驳道。

"No arguing," I said in a tone that meant exactly that.

The kids **piled into**[1] the car. "You're going to see just how much time those who care about you spend when they give you a present." I told them. Handing Drew a pad of paper and a pencil, I said, "Please mark down the time we left home."

When we reached town, Drew noted our arrival time. The children helped me select presents for my sisters at a local shop. Then we turned round and drove home.

Bursting free from the confines of the car, the children headed for their yard toys. "Not so fast," I said. "We've got to wrap the presents." The kids slouched inside.

"Drew," I asked, "did you note the time we got home?" He nodded. "OK, please time the girls while they wrap the presents."

When they'd tied the last bow, they looked up expectantly. "How long did this all take?" I asked Drew.

Glancing at his notes, he said, "It took us 28 minutes to get to town and 15 minutes to buy the presents. Then it was 38 minutes to get home because we had to buy petrol."

"And how long did it take us to wrap the boxes?" Eleanor asked.

"Each of you did one present in two minutes," Drew said.

"And how many minutes will it take to mail these presents?" I asked.

"Fifty-six minutes, round trip," Drew reckoned.

"But you forgot standing-in-line time, "said Sarah.

"OK," Drew said. "We need to add about 15 minutes for mailing."

① pile into 挤入，进入

“别吵。”我以一种不容置疑的口吻命令道。

孩子们一个个挤进汽车。“你们会明白，那些关心你们的人为了给你们送礼物，到底花了多少时间。”我对他们说。我交给德鲁一叠纸和一支铅笔，告诉他，“记下我们离家的时间。”

到了镇上，德鲁又记下我们抵达的时间。在当地一家商店里，孩子们帮我为我的几个姐姐挑选礼物。之后我们调转头，开车回家。

孩子们从车里跑出来，径直朝着放有玩具的院子里冲去。“别这么急，”我说，“我们还要包装礼物呢。”他们只好没精打采地回到屋。

“德鲁，你记下我们到家的时间了吗？”我问。他点点头。“那好，现在请记录她们两个女孩子包礼物的时间。”

她们打好最后一个蝴蝶结后，充满期待地抬起头来。“总共花了多少时间？”我问德鲁。

他看了看记录，说，“我们花了 28 分钟进城，15 分钟买礼物；之后用了 38 分钟回家，因为途中给汽车加油了。”

“包好这些礼盒用了多少时间？”埃莉诺问。

“你们各自包好一件礼物需要 2 分钟。”德鲁回答。

“把这些礼物寄出去要用多长时间？”我问。

“来回 56 分钟。”德鲁推算了一下。

“可你忘了排队的时间。”萨拉说。

“对，”德鲁答道，“我们还要多加上 15 分钟。”

"So, what's the total time we'd spend to give someone a present?"

Drew worked out the arithmetic. "Two hours and 34 minutes," he said.

I laid some stationery, a pen and an envelope beside each child. "Now please write a thank-you note. Be sure to mention the present by name and tell what fun you'll have using it."

Silence reigned as the children gathered their thoughts; soft pen scratchings followed. "Done," said Eleanor, pressing her envelope closed.

"Me too." echoed Sarah.

"That took us three minutes." Drew said, sealing his letter.

"Is three minutes too much to thank someone for a thoughtful gift that may have taken two-and-a-half hours to choose and send to you?" I asked.

The children looked down at the table and shook their heads.

"It's a good idea to get into the habit now. In time you'll want to write thank-you notes for many things."

Drew groaned. "Like what?"

"Like dinners or lunches. Or weekends at someone's home or the time someone takes to give you advice on university applications or careers."

"Did you have to write thank-yous when you were a kid?" Drew asked.

"Absolutely."

"What did you say?" he asked. I could tell he was formulating the rest of his thank-you notes.

"It was a long time ago," I said.

Then I remembered Uncle Arthur, my great-grandfather's youngest brother. I'd never met him, yet every Christmas he sent me a gift. He was blind and lived far away. His niece Becca, who lived next door, sat down with him and wrote out

“那么，送给别人一件礼物一共要花多少时间？”

德鲁很快算了出来，“2 小时 34 分。”

我在每个孩子面前放上信纸、钢笔和信封。“现在，请各写一封感谢信。务必写上礼物的名字，还有它将会带给你的快乐。”

孩子们聚精会神，寂静无声；接着只听到钢笔书写的沙沙声。“写好了。”埃莉诺一边说，一边封上信口。

“我也写好了。”萨拉随后说。

“这花了我们 3 分钟。”德鲁说话的当儿把信封上。

“花 3 分钟来感谢别人可能花了两个半小时为你们精心挑选和邮寄礼物的时间，这多吗？”我问。

孩子们低头望着桌子，纷纷摇头。

“现在就养成写感谢信的习惯，这可是个不错的主意。总有一天，你们会因为各种事情想到要写感谢信的。”

德鲁轻轻问了一句，“比如什么？”

“比如因为晚餐或者午宴，或者在别人家里过周末，或者有人花时间为你求学和就职当参谋。”

“你小时候也要写感谢信吗？”德鲁问。

“当然！”

“你写些什么？”他继续问道。我看得出，他正在套写其他几封感谢信。

“那是很久以前的事了。”我说。

接着我记起了阿瑟叔公，他是我曾祖父最小的兄弟。我从未见过他，可每年圣诞节我都会收到他寄来的礼物。他双目失明，住在很远的地方。他的侄女贝凯住在他隔壁，常常过去坐在他身边，帮他给他所有的侄孙女、

$5 cheques to his great—and great-great-grandnieces and—nephews. I always wrote, telling him what I'd spent his cheque on.

Years later, I had the chance to visit Uncle Arthur. As we chatted, he told me he'd always enjoyed my notes.

"You remember them?" I asked.

"Yes," he replied. "I've saved some of my favorites." He waved towards a stand by the window. "Would you get the packet of letters out of the top drawer? It's wrapped in ribbon."

I found an old letter with my handwriting and read aloud: "Dear Uncle Arthur, I am writing this to you as I sit under the hair dryer at the beauty salon. Tonight is the Holiday Ball at the high school and I am spending your Christmas cheque having my hair done for the party. Thank you so very much. I know I'll have a wonderful time, in part because of your thoughtful gift. Love, Faith."

"And did you?" he asked.

I thought back to that wonderful evening so many years ago. "Definitely," I answered with a smile that I wished Uncle Arthur could see.

Sarah's tug at my sleeve pulled me back to the present. "What are you smiling at?" she asked.

I told the children about Uncle Arthur's gifts and how glad I was that I'd written a note each year. They obviously meant a lot to him.

"And did you look beautiful?" Asked Sarah.

"My date thought I did."

"Who did you go to the ball with? What did you wear?" asked Eleanor.

"I think I have a photo of that evening," I said, going to the bookshelves and pulling down a scrapbook. I opened it to a photo of me standing in front of

曾侄孙女和侄子填写 5 美元的支票。我总是给他回信，告诉他我已把他寄来的支票派何用场。

多年以后，我终于有机会去探望他。我们一起闲聊的时候，他告诉我他一直都很喜欢我写给他的信。

“您还记得那些信呀？”我问。

“记得，”他回答道，“我珍藏了几封我最喜欢的。”他指了指窗户旁边的一架立柜，“最上面那个抽屉里有一扎，用丝带捆着的，拿过来好吗？”

我找出一封我写的旧信，大声读了起来：“亲爱的阿瑟叔公，我坐在美容院里的吹风机下给您写这封信。今晚学校要举行假日舞会，我正用您圣诞节寄来的支票在这儿做头发，好出席这台晚会。我要对您表达诚挚的谢意。我知道，今晚我会度过一段美好的时光，部分原因就是有您送我的这么体贴周到的礼物。爱您。”

“那天晚上你玩得开心吗？”他问。

我便回想起多年前那个美丽的夜晚。“当然。”我微笑地回答。我真希望阿瑟叔公能看到我的笑靥。

萨拉使劲拽了一下我的衣袖，把我带回眼前的现实。“你笑什么？”她问。

我就告诉孩子们有关阿瑟叔公给我寄礼物的事，并说我有多么高兴，因为我每年都给他写了回信。那些信对他来说显然十分有意义。

“当年你看上去很漂亮吗？”萨拉问。

“我的约会对象觉得我很漂亮。”

“那场舞会你同谁一起去的？你穿的什么衣服？”埃莉诺接着问道。

“我想，我有一张那个晚上的照片。”我一边说，一边走向书架，取下一本剪贴簿。我打开相簿，翻到我的一张照片，照片里我正站在我父母的

my parents' fireplace. I'm wearing a black velvet evening dress, and my hair is done in an elaborate French twist. Beside me, a handsome young man beams as he hands me a corsage.

"But that's Daddy!" Eleanor said with surprise.

I nodded and smiled.

As the children settled down to finish the rest of their notes, I stroked the faded petals of the dried gardenia pasted next to the photo.

Last Christmas, Bob and I celebrated our thirty-sixth wedding anniversary. Thank you, Uncle Arthur.

壁炉前面。我穿着一身黑色的天鹅绒晚礼服，头发做成精心设计的法国式卷发。我的身边站着一位英俊的年轻小伙，他满面笑容地递给我一束胸花。

“这不就是爸爸嘛！”埃莉诺吃惊地叫了起来。

我点点头，满脸微笑。

孩子们又安下心去写他们没写完的感谢信，我轻轻抚摸着贴在照片旁边早已褪色的栀子花瓣。

就在去年圣诞节，我和鲍勃庆祝了我们结婚 36 周年纪念日。谢谢您，阿瑟叔公。

Do One Thing Every Day that Scares You
每天做一件自己害怕的事

◎ Eleanor Roosevelt

Fear comes from the fact that you think you cannot act or will act incorrectly. But if you actually try, even though you're scared as hell, you'll often realize that these fears didn't have any foundations. They can be blown away if you tell yourself you'll just do it whatever happens. In many cases you'll think that death is your worse case, but you have to realize you're over-exaggerating.

It's crazy how much our brain can work in order to protect us against ourselves. Imagine you're in a plane, about to jump out of it to do some **parachuting**[①]. You've never done that before. When you're about to jump, the brain jumps in and start giving you every bit of information it has against parachuting because fear has a seed into you brain. But if you've been jumping out of airplanes for ages, let me tell you the brain simply doesn't care anymore because it knows nothing will (generally) happen. This concept is the **core**[②] idea of doing one thing that scares you every day.

When you push your limits, the number of fears you have start to decrease. With time you will start understanding that all those fears are just crap that your brain creates to protect you from the unknown but you'll also know that this

① parachuting ['pærəʃu:tiŋ] n. 跳伞，空降
② core [kɔ:] n. 核心，要义

美丽语录

Fear is the only thing that limits you from acting what you want to act. Don't let those fears control you for all your life, start showing them who's the real boss here.

恐惧是唯一一件阻扰你去做想要做的事情的东西。不要让这些恐惧控制你一生，让它们瞧瞧谁才是你命运的真正主人。

当你认为你无法完成或者会搞砸一件事的时候，恐惧就会产生。但是，如果你真正去尝试，你会经常意识到，那种恐惧其实是毫无依据的，尽管你当时害怕得要死。如果你告诉自己，不管发生什么，我就是要这样做，恐惧就会消失得无影无踪。许多情况下，你会认为死亡是最坏的情况，但是你必须要意识到，你有点夸大其词了。

为了保护自己，我们的大脑会不顾一切地让我们去做事与愿违的事。想象一下，你在一架飞机中正准备跳伞，可你以前从未跳过。这时，大脑会灌输一些负面信息让你无法顺利跳伞，因为恐惧像种子那样扎根在我们的头脑中。假如你此前有几年跳伞经历的话，我可以告诉你，你的大脑不会有所顾忌，因为你知道通常不会有意外发生。这个概念是“每天做一件你害怕的事”的核心理念。

当你将自己推向能力极限的时候，让你感到恐惧的事就会开始减少。

unknown is not that dangerous. Approaching girls on the street is something many guys are just going to freeze if they have to do it, but it is possible. It just takes time and effort. If you do it one step at a time you'll realize that there's nothing really dangerous about doing it.

What is really interesting from doing this technique every day is that you experience a good amount of adrenaline through your body. It's also really great to have done something you thought you couldn't do. Doing this will make your life at least a thousand time better because there won't be any barriers to stop you. You'll get a better life, more respect from your peers, more control over yourself and will be able to share lots of experiences other might never thought about doing because they are too scared to follow the "Do one thing every day that scares you" mentality. But you are strong.

If you do things you think shouldn't be doing, sometimes you get opposite results: you get what you were looking for. Take this example: you put money into a saving account which gives you a poor return rate but you do so because you are "scared" of losing your money. You decide it's time to apply your new mentality and take the money and start buying shares instead. Maybe for the first transactions you'll have a bit of a rush/adrenaline going on because you aren't sure of what's going to happen, but then you are really proud of what you did. Even though you might have made mistakes, by doing what you were afraid of you removed a barrier you had. As time goes by, you learn how the market works and you'll get better. You'll might even make thousands of thousand by doing it. And now you're really happy because you got past what you were looking for: earning something with the money you had. What the real accomplishment is, is that you've shown to yourself you were able to get over a fear you had. Amazing.

久而久之，你会渐渐领悟，其实所有的恐惧都是在事情未知时，你的大脑出于保护自己的本能而产生的，而且你也会领悟到那些未知的事情没有那么危险。在街上慢慢接近女孩，这个举动会让许多男孩手足无措，但这并不是无法办到的事。只是要花费一点时间和努力。如果你一步一个脚印地做事，你会发现，所谓的危险其实没什么大不了。

每天做这样一件技术活的有趣之处，就是你体内会产生大量的肾上腺素。而且假如你完成了原先你认为做不到的事，你会感觉非常棒。这样做至少可以让你的生活好上一千倍以上，因为不会再有任何障碍阻止你。你会过上更好的生活，获得同行们更多的尊敬，而且你能更好地控制自己，能够分享许多别人想都不敢想的经历，因为他们太害怕以至于没有“每天做一件你畏惧的事”的心态。但是你很坚强。

如果你做一些你原本认为不应该做的事，有时你会得到相反的结果：你得到了你渴望的东西。比如：你把钱存入回报率很低的储蓄账户，因为你害怕损失钱财。于是你觉得是时候要改变心态，把钱取出来转而买进股票。也许在第一轮交易中你会莽撞行事，肾上腺素会跟着上升，因为你不知道会发生什么，但是接着你会对你所做的事感到非常自豪。尽管你可能会犯错误，但一次次坚持做自己害怕的事，你会为自己扫清障碍。随着时间推移，你会渐渐明白市场是怎么运作的，你会越来越好。你甚至可能成千上百次地去做这件事。现在你真正地感到幸福，因为你得到了你渴望已久的东西：用自己的钱去投资并获得回报。真正的成就是什么，是你已经证明自己可以克服恐惧了。太棒了。

A Lesson on Mental Clutter

如何清理心灵垃圾

◎ Erin

In the children's book Zen Shorts by Jon Muth, a giant panda named Stillwater tells three stories to young siblings Addy, Michael, and Karl. All of the stories are famous Buddhist teachings, and you may be familiar with them even if you haven't seen this beautifully illustrated book.

The third story Stillwater shares with Karl is called "A Heavy Load" and is about two traveling monks. During their journey, two monks come upon an awful woman who refuses to cross a river because she does not wish to get her silken robes wet or dirty. The older of the two monks quickly picks up the woman and carries her across the water. Many hours later, the younger monk is very upset and visibly angry about his friend helping someone so disdainful, and he feels obliged to share his frustration with the older monk:

"That woman back there was very selfish and rude, but you picked her up on your back and carried her! Then she didn't even thank you!"

"I set the woman down hours ago," the older monk replied. "Why are you still carrying her?"

I think of this story whenever I find a dirty cup in our television room or

美丽语录

Before you talk, listen; before you react, think; before you quit, try.

在你说话之前，先听；在你回应之前，先想；在你退出之前，先试。

在乔恩·马斯给孩子们写的《禅宗小故事》一书中，一个名叫“静水”的大熊猫给他的弟弟妹妹安迪、迈克尔和卡尔讲了三个故事。这些故事都是著名的佛教教义，即使你还没有读过这本精美的图画书，里面的故事你可能已经颇为熟悉了。

静水讲给卡尔的第三个故事叫做《沉重的包袱》，是关于两个和尚旅行途中的故事。有一天，两个和尚碰到一位让人头疼的妇女，她因为怕弄湿或弄脏自己的丝裙而拒绝过河。年长的和尚立刻背起这个妇女过了河。过了几个小时，年轻的和尚对这件事耿耿于怀，并且怒形于色。他觉得自己的同伴不应该帮助这个令人鄙视的妇女，决定一定要把自己的不快告知同伴。

“那个女人既自私又粗鲁，你还要背她过河！她甚至连声谢谢都没说！”

“几个小时前我就把她放下了，”年长的和尚回答说，“你却为何一直放不下？”

每当我在客厅里看到用过没洗的水杯，或丢在地板上而不是篮子里的

clothing on the floor instead of in the hamper or notice that a co-worker dropped the ball on a small task. I remind myself that I have two options—I can be like the young monk and throw a fit and be in a bad mood and let it annoy me for hours, or I can be like the older monk and take care of the problem myself and immediately let go of the frustration. I get to decide if I want the cup or errant sock or unfinished task to **clutter up**[①] my mind and put me in a bad mood, and, since I'd rather not have that clutter wasting my time and energy, I usually choose to be like the older monk.

I'm not a maid—and I'm not suggesting you become one either—but I get to decide how I'm going to react to a situation. Remembering, too, that I don't know the full story behind why the glass or sock is out of place or why a task at work was left unfinished. For all I know, my co-worker got an important call from a client and had to stop a project mid-way through completion to handle an emergency. By helping out, instead of getting frustrated and throwing a fit, I'm making the situation better for myself and others. I get to choose not to fill my time with more clutter than the small item I **encountered**[②].

That said, if there is a persistent habit of other people leaving messes in their work, a conversation about that behavior is certainly in order. However, frustrations caused by occasional messes are usually not worth carrying around with you and cluttering up your mind, energy, and emotions.

① clutter up 使杂乱，散乱

② encounter [in'kauntə] v. 遭遇，遇到

脏衣服，或者看到同事有一些小任务没能完成，我都会想到这个故事。我提醒自己，我有两个选择——可以像那个年轻的和尚一样发脾气，让坏情绪烦扰自己，或者选择像那个年长的和尚一样自己解决问题，不让坏情绪跟着自己。我必须决定是否让那个没洗的杯子、乱丢的袜子或是没完成的任务来困扰我，影响我的心情。我并不情愿让这些负面情绪浪费我的时间和精力，我通常选择那个年长和尚的做法。

我不是个女佣，我也不希望你也变成这样，但我必须决定我如何应对这些情况。而且要记住，我不知道到底为什么杯子或者袜子被乱放，也不知道那个任务究竟为什么没有完成。我只知道，我的同事接到一个重要的客户电话，不得不停下手中的工作去处理一件急事。与其生气发脾气，不如帮助他完成那个任务，这样对我和他都有好处。所以我选择去完成这些小的任务，而不是浪费时间在生气上。

也就是说，如果有些人养成了给别人制造麻烦的习惯，就必须有人找他们谈谈。不过，偶尔的不注意一般就不值得耿耿于怀了，这样做只能扰乱自己的心灵、能量和情绪。

Sow the Seed, See the Harvest

撒下种子，期盼收获

◎ Steve Brunkhorst

The story is told of two boys who were walking through a field and found some corn seeds **scattered**[①] across the ground. They each took one of the seeds home and planted it.

When the first boy didn't see a tiny **sprout**[②] after the second day, he dug up the seed to see if it had sprouted. Each day he dug up the seed and replanted it, but the corn would not grow. The seed had germinated; yet the boy had not allowed it to maintain contact with the soil, take root, and obtain nutrients. So, it died.

The second boy planted his seed and left it alone. He imagined a tall stalk of corn where he had planted the seed. He waited patiently as rains came and sunshine bathed the ground with warmth. In ten days, a small sprout had broken through the ground, its curled leaves reaching toward the sky.

Achieving any desire, whether large or small, begins with a seed sown in the mind. That seed is the vision of its fulfillment. It also requires the

① scattered ['skætəd] adj. 散乱的，散布的

② sprout [spraut] v. 发芽，抽条

美丽语录

Just sow your seed, allow it to grow, and see an abundant harvest.

播下种子，让它成长，期待丰收，这就可以了。

这是一个关于两个男孩的故事。他俩穿过一片田地时，发现一些散落在地上的玉米种子。他们每人捡了一粒，带回家种在了土里。

第二天，第一个男孩见种子还没有发出芽来，便把种子从土里挖了出来，看看它到底有没有发芽。每一天他都要把种子挖出来，然后再重新种上，但是种子始终不长。其实，种子已经发芽了，但是男孩总不让它与土壤接触，结果种子无法生根、吸收养分，便死了。

第二个男孩把种子种上后，就没再打扰它。他想象着他播下种子的地方会长出一株茁壮高大的玉米。不管是下雨，还是温暖阳光沐浴大地，他都耐心地等待着。10 天后，一个嫩芽破土而出，它那卷曲的叶子伸向天空。

任何愿望的实现，不管其大小，都始于我们心灵中播下的那颗种子。那里种子能勾勒出愿望实现时的景象，但它需要我们耐心等待这一景象成

commitment to allow the vision to grow. Commitment in daily life allows life's storms to strengthen resolve. Resolve allows us to nurture a new dream, improve an existing dream, or even begin over if necessary.

How often do we plant the seed of a beautiful dream in the fertile soil of our minds, and then dig it up? What could you achieve if you allowed your seed to grow, continuing to focus your spiritual eyes on the harvest?

为现实。日常生活中，如果我们尽心尽力，生活中的暴风雨只会加强我们的决心，而决心会使我们滋养新的梦想，完善已有的梦想，甚至在必要时重新再来。

我们在心灵的沃土中播下一颗美好梦想的种子后，不待它生根发芽就将它掘出土壤，这样的事情多久我们就会做一次呢？如果你让种子生长，不断将你心灵的眼睛投向那丰收时的景象，你会收获什么呢？

Are You Ignoring That Little Thought
你在忽略那些小想法吗

◎ Caroline Jalango

What happened to that brilliant idea that you once had? Did you ignore it because you thought that it was just a little thought?

Have you ever considered what that little thought would have become if you had acted on your instincts or if you had paid more attention to it?

Imagine a **scenario**①, where you are sitting at home watching television or reading a book, suddenly a light buld is turned on in the dark tunnel of your mind as a thought or an idea crosses your mind. The thought catches your attention but seems so meaningless and you are tempted to discard it, but wait a minute!

That thought could be the potential beginning of the success you have so mush yearned for. As the thought crosses your mind, your senses become alert and you suddenly see a possibility, a realization, a solution, a conclusion, or find the answer to a problem whose solution has long **eluded**② you.

It is almost as if a divine being has whispered the perfect solution into your ear or awakened your senses to a reality thereby bringing illumination to your

---

① scenario [si'nɑ:riəu] n. 情节，场景，局面

② elude [i'lu:d] v. 躲避，逃避；使困惑

美丽语录

Give everything a shot. You never know what (or who) is going to change your life.

任何事情都应该去尝试一下，因为你无法知道，什么样的事或者什么样的人将会改变你的一生。

你曾经想到过的那个非凡的主意后来怎样了？你是否因为觉得那只是个小小的念头而将其忽略了呢?

你是否考虑过，如果你依照直觉行事，或是多用点心，当初那个小小的念头将会变成怎样?

想象这样一个场景：你正坐在家里看电视或看书，一个想法或念头闪过脑际，令你眼前一亮，豁然开朗。这个想法虽然令你心中为之一动，但却似乎毫无意义，于是你打算放弃它。但是请等一下！

那个想法可能就是你渴望已久的潜在的成功起点。当它在你头脑中闪过时，你的思维变得敏锐起来，你突然看到了一种可能性、一种想法的实现、一个解决方案、一个结论，或是找到让你困惑已久的问题的答案。

这就像是一位圣人在你耳边低语，告诉你最佳的解决方案，或者将你的思维唤回到现实，从而给你的人生带来光明。这就像是找到智力拼图的

life. It is like finding the last piece of jigsaw puzzle.

This becomes an AHA moment and everything freezes around you as you excitedly try to grasp the practicality of that little but powerful thought.

Your self-confidence and enthusiasm increase as you become conscious of the great possibilities that can arise if that little thought is acted upon. This becomes the moment to build upon that thought and to write down any ideas that are streaming from that little thought for later review.

Seemingly meaningless little thought or ideas when acted upon have a potential to explode into great projects.

Many successful projects have been born from the little positive thoughts that were carefully nurtured and recognized as tickets to great things.

You may have heard people say many times that it just came to me in a flash, in a flash moment , a small idea or seemingly meaningless thought may cross your mind about something you have been planning to accomplish .

Don't waste an opportunity to act on a potentially brilliant idea. You don't have to wait for a major idea, a master strategy, or approval from your peers in order for you to act on that little thought.

That little thought or idea is the beginning of great things if you decide to follow it through.

最后一块一样。

这将成为一个令人惊喜的时刻。当你满心激动，努力领会那个不起眼但非常有用的想法的实用性时，周围的一切都好像静止了。

当你意识到，如果实践那个小小的想法，就会产生极大的可能性时，你的自信心就会增强，热情也会高涨。此时，你要以那个小小的想法为基础，记下由其激发出的所有念头，以便日后回顾。

看似无足轻重的小想法或念头一旦得以实施，就具有演变成伟大事业的潜能。

许多成功的事业都源于那些得到精心孕育的积极的小想法，这些想法被看作是走向辉宏事业的敲门砖。

你可能听别人多次说过：我瞬间有了那个想法。闪念之间，一个与你一直计划实现的事情有关的小点子或看似毫无意义的想法，就可能会在你脑中闪过。

不要浪费任何一个实践某个充满潜力的非凡念头的机会。你不必为了实践那个小念头而等待大主意、总体规划的出现，或是等待同伴的赞同。

如果你下定决心坚持到底，那个小小的想法或念头就会是你成就伟大事业的开始。

Why Should You Forgive Yourself
为什么你必须原谅自己

◎ Marc

Once upon a time there lived a woman who had a bad temper. She screamed at and scolded everyone around her. For most of her life she believed the **fiery**① rage inside her was everyone else's fault.

She went to see a well respected Buddhist monk to ask for advice. The monk told her to take a large clay jug from his kitchen, fill it with water, and stand outside on the sidewalk in front of his house. "It's hot outside, and that's a busy sidewalk with lots of **pedestrians**②," the monk told her as he pointed out the front window of his house. "When a pedestrian passes, you must offer them a glass of water. Do this until there is no rage left inside you."

So she stood outside with a water jug and served water to pedestrians every day for the next several weeks. And every morning she asked herself if rage still pulsed through her veins. And every morning the answer was, "yes." So she continued serving water. Until this afternoon when a burly man walked up, snatched the water jug out of her hand, drank directly out of it, and then tossed

---

① fiery ['faiəri] adj. 火一般的，激烈的

② pedestrian [pi'destriən] n. 行人，步行者

美丽语录

To forgive is to set a prisoner free and discover the prisoner was you.

原谅就是释放囚徒，然后发现那囚徒不是别人，正是自己。

从前有个脾气很坏的女人，她总是对周围的每一个人大吼大叫。大多数时候，她都认为自己的愤怒全是因为别人的错。

于是，她去向一个德高望重的高僧讨教。高僧让她从厨房取了一个很大的陶壶，装满水，提着站在房前外面的人行道上。“外面很热，行人很多。”高僧指着窗户外说，“每一个行人经过你身边时，你都要给他们一杯水，直到你心中没有愤怒为止。”

所以，在接下来的几周里，她都拿着陶壶站在外面，给过往行人提供水。每天早晨，她都问自己，心中是否还有愤怒，而每天她的回答都是肯定的。于是她继续这样做着，直到有一天下午，一个粗鲁的男人走过来，一把从她手里抢过陶壶，一口气喝完了里面的水，把壶扔在地上，径直离开。

the jug on the ground as he continued on his way.

The rage within the woman skyrocketed into an irrepressible fit. Unable to contain herself, she picked up the clay jug off the ground and, with all her might, threw it at the burly man as he walked away. It was a direct hit. The jug shattered into pieces over the back of his head and he fell to the ground, unconscious and bleeding.

As the woman's rage subsided, she realized the magnitude of what she had done and began to cry. She used a payphone to call 911 and report the incident. An ambulance and two police cars arrived at the scene moments later. As the EMTs strapped the burly man into a stretcher, the police handcuffed his arms and legs to the stretcher. Then one of the police officers walked over to the woman, who was still crying, and said, "The city owes you a big 'thank you.' That man has been on our most wanted list for over a year now. He is a primary suspect in multiple murder cases and violent robberies."

The moral of the story is that we simply don't know. We want to believe that if we completely rid ourselves of our inner darkness then we will always make the right choices, and be of service to ourselves and those around us. But life isn't so linear and predicable. Sometimes our darkness inadvertently leads us to do things that impact the world in a positive way, just as our unconditional love sometimes forces us to overlook the criminal standing before us.

女人怒火中烧，终于抑制不住怒气发作起来。无法控制自己的她捡起地上的陶壶，用尽全力掷向那个男人。陶壶直接砸中了男人的后脑勺，陶壶摔成碎片，男人倒在地上不省人事，流血不止。

女人的怒气平息了，也意识到自己犯了一个多么大的错，于是哭了起来。她用公用电话叫了 911，报告了这起事故。不久，一辆救护车和两辆警车来到现场。救护人员把那个粗鲁的男人抬上了担架，警察也拷上了那名男子的手脚。然后，一个警察走到哭泣的女人身边，说，“整个城市要向你郑重地道谢。那个男人是一年多来我们的头号通缉犯。他是多起抢劫杀人案的首要嫌疑人。”

这个故事的寓意是我们无法简单得知的。我们总是愿意相信，当我们完全摆脱内心的黑暗后，我们才能做出对的选择，才会对我们自己和身边的人都有好处。但生活并不是这么线性及可预测的。有时我们内心的黑暗会无意中指使我们做一些影响世界的积极的事，就像我们无条件的爱，时常会让我们忽略那些近在咫尺的罪恶。

A Letter to My Future Self
写给未来自己的一封信

◎ Sherri

In 1994, I wrote a letter. I stuck it in an envelope, put it away and completely forgot about it.

It wasn't until we moved into our new home in 2006 that I found it again. It was addressed to me with **explicit**[①] instructions not to open until my birthday 2005. It was now 2006 so I decided to open it. This is what it said:

Dear Sherri,

By the time you read this you will be 30. At the age of 18 I had so many hopes and dreams about where you'd be, what you'd be doing and with whom you'd spend your life with.

Right now I hope that you have traveled and seen everything you've always wanted to, both in Canada and overseas, and maybe even settled down somewhere in Australia doing some research in the field of biology (genetics).

I hope you're married to the man of your dreams. The man of mine is Gwynn. He is originally from South Africa (another place I wish to visit).

You'll probably have two children of your own—a girl(Michaela Anne) and a boy (name yet to be decided).

① explicit [iks'plisit] adj. 详尽的，清楚的

美丽语录

Never give up your dreams. Miracles happen every day.

别放弃梦想，奇迹每天都在上演。

1994 年，我写了一封信。我把它装进信封收起来，就完全忘记了。

直到 2006 年我们搬到新家，我才又发现了这封信。收信人是我自己，而且明确说明一定到 2005 年我生日的时候才能打开，那时候已经是 2006 年，所以我决定打开它。信里这样写道：

亲爱的雪莉：

你读这封信的时候已经 30 岁了。18 岁的我有太多关于未来的希望和梦想，你会在哪里生活，你会做什么工作，你会和谁共度一生。

我希望你已经去过了所有你想去的地方，看过了所有你感兴趣的东西，不管是在加拿大还是国外。也许，现在你已经在澳大利亚的某处定居，做着生物学（遗传学）领域的研究工作。

我希望你已经嫁给了你的梦中情人。我的梦中情人叫格温，他来自南非（另一个我心神往之的地方）。

你应该有了两个自己的孩子：一个男孩一个女孩。女孩叫安妮，男孩的名字还没想好。

If everything goes according to plan you'll be living in Australia in a big house in a small town outside of a big city with a lot of land, a dog, Gwynn and your two beautiful children. Hopefully you have a career in the medical field, maybe doing research in genetics. Gwynn will be a computer programmer and you will be doing alright for yourselves.

However, if things don't go according to plan for you, I wish you all the love, happiness and joy in the world and don't settle for anything less than the best since that is absolutely what you deserve.

Live long, be happy and live life to it's fullest.

Love Sherri "18"

When I read this for the first time since writing it I was floored. Even now having dug this up again another 4 years later I still can't help but think this is really cool.

So much of what I wanted for myself has materialized.

I did travel to a few more places in Canada although I haven't seen everything I'd like to.

I did marry the man of my dreams and yes he still is my one and only.

I've traveled to the UK, South Africa, Australia and New Zealand.

I lived in Australia for nearly 4 years in a big house, in a small suburb, in a major city (close enough).

I had a career in Biology in the field of genetics for 10 years.

I have two lovely kids—both boys (names now decided).

I have not one dog but two dogs. Both yellow labs from Australia.

Gwynn is a computer programmer.

We are doing okay for ourselves.

如果一切按计划进行，那现在的你会和格温还有两个漂亮的孩子，一起生活在澳大利亚某个大城市外的小镇上，有一个大房子，有很多地，养一只狗。希望你是从事医学领域的工作，也可能是做遗传学研究。格温会是计算机程序员，你们一切都很好。

不过，就算生活没有按你的计划进行，我也祝你拥有世上所有的爱、幸福和快乐。在遇到最好的之前，别让自己停下来，你绝对值得拥有最好的生活。

多福多寿，要快乐，要活到最精彩。

爱你的：18 岁的雪莉

自写信到第一次读这封信的时候，我诧异不已。即使 4 年后的今天再次拿出来读，我也还是觉得这真的是很酷的想法。

那么多我想要的都已经实现了。

我真的去过加拿大很多地方旅行，虽然我还没把想看的东西通通看过。

我嫁给了我的梦中情人，对，他依旧是我的唯一。

我去过英国、南非、澳大利亚和新西兰。

我在澳大利亚的一个大城市生活了快四年，我们住在郊区的大房子里（跟梦想很接近了）。

我有一份生物学遗传领域的工作，干了 10 年了。

我有两个可爱的孩子——不过都是男孩（名字都定了）。

我现在养着两只狗，都是产自澳大利亚的黄色拉布拉多，跟信中写的那只稍有不同。

格温是计算机程序员。

我们一切都好。

After writing this I quickly forgot about what I had put in here actually. The things that materialized were all met with quite a bit of **resistance**① (all internal) but I suppose these were things that I really did want. Having never strayed too far from home, overseas travel was a huge deal. Having never been away from my family, moving to Australia for several years was an incredibly huge decision.

I find it fascinating how the dreams of a young and naive little girl can become a grown woman's reality.

I'm curious if you guys have ever written anything to your future self and how it **stacks up**② to your current reality. If you haven't, will you join me in writing a letter now to yourself in say 10 years from now? It's an interesting little experiment.

① resistance [ri'zistəns] n. 阻碍，阻力，反抗

② stack up 成为结果

其实写完这篇文章我就很快忘了自己写了什么。所有我实现的梦想，都曾经遭遇了一些内心的阻碍，但是我很确定，这些就是我想要的。对于从未离家太远的我来说，出国旅行是大事。对于从未离开过家人的我来说，搬到澳大利亚住几年也是难以置信的重大决定。

看着一个年轻而天真的小女孩的梦想成为一个成熟女人的真实生活，这个感觉很美好。

我很好奇，你们有没有给未来的自己写过什么，然后看着它们一点点堆积成为你现在的生活。如果还没写过，那不如加入我，现在拿起笔，给十年后的自己写封信吧？这可是一次有趣的小实验。

阅读小课堂

What the "ABC" Tell US
26个字母——人生哲理篇

A—Acknowledging（感激）

感激你所拥有的一切。

B—Belief（信念）

做任何一件事情，都要有坚定的信念。

C—Confidence（信心）

对自己充满信心。

D—Dreaming（梦想）

今日带着梦想入睡，明天带着梦想醒来。

E—Empathy（心灵相通）

站在对方的立场上，为对方着想。

F—Fun（乐趣）

享受你所拥有的一切。

G—Giving（给予）

将你所能给予的都给予你周围的人。

H—Happiness（幸福观）

为你的生活及所做的事感到满意。

I—Imagination（想象力）

张开想象的翅膀，追求你的梦想。

J—Joy（欢乐）

把你的欢乐带给你所认识的人。

K—Knowledge（知识）

不断学习各种知识。

L—Love（爱心）

奉献你的爱心及爱的精神。

M—Motivation（激励）

不断激励自己，实现自我超越。

N—Nice（友善）

即使对陌生人也保持一颗善心。

O—Openness（开化）

敞开胸怀，接受新事物。

P—Patience（耐心）

坚持就是胜利，耐心等待成功出现。

Q—Quiet（安宁）

享受安宁的时光，静下心来反省自己。

R—Respect（尊重）

尊重所有的种族、宗教、文化、信仰及价值观。

S—Smile（微笑）

用微笑面对人生。

T—Trust（信任）

信任自己的亲朋好友和其他值得你信任的人。

U—Unity（团结）

与周围的人和平相处。

V—Victory（成功）

庆祝自己的成功，即便是最微小的成就。

W—Wait（等候）

耐心等候，好运总会出现。

X—Xfactor（未知因数）

挖掘自己身上未知的潜力，看到别人身上隐藏的光芒。

Y—Yes（赞同）

迎接积极的挑战，敢于面对一切。

Z—Zest（极大的生活乐趣）

把所有的事情都做到最好，尽力而为，感受最真实的生活。

Life is a pure flame, and we live

by an invisile sun within us.

生命是束纯净的火焰，

我们依靠自己内心看不见的太阳而存在